LEAD WITH PURPOSE LIKE ANAND MAHINDRA

Rajiv Agarwal is a family business consultant with more than twenty years of experience. Considered a leading expert on family business in India, he has advised more than 1,500 families on succession, strategy and continuity. Currently a professor of Family Business, Strategy and Entrepreneurship at SP Jain Institute of Management & Research (SPJIMR), Mumbai, which is also his alma mater, Agarwal is an alumnus of BITS Pilani and Harvard Business School. He has been the visiting professor at IIM Kozhikode and IIM Indore, and expert advisor on the Board of Academics, Department of Management, Nirma University, Ahmedabad.

Also by the same author

Think, Lead & Strategize Like Kumar Mangalam Birla

LEAD WITH PURPOSE LIKE ANAND MAHINDRA

RAJIV AGARWAL

RUPA

Published by
Rupa Publications India Pvt. Ltd 2019
7/16, Ansari Road, Daryaganj
New Delhi 110002

Sales centres:
Allahabad Bengaluru Chennai
Hyderabad Jaipur Kathmandu
Kolkata Mumbai

Copyright © Rajiv Agarwal 2019

The views and opinions expressed in this book are the author's own and
the facts are as reported by him which have been
verified to the extent possible, and the publishers are not in
any way liable for the same.

All rights reserved.

No part of this publication may be reproduced, transmitted,
or stored in a retrieval system, in any form or by any means,
electronic, mechanical, photocopying, recording or otherwise,
without the prior permission of the publisher.

ISBN: 978-93-5333-504-5

First impression 2019

10 9 8 7 6 5 4 3 2 1

The moral right of the author has been asserted.

Printed at Nutech Print Services, Faridabad

This book is sold subject to the condition that it shall not,
by way of trade or otherwise, be lent, resold, hired out, or otherwise
circulated, without the publisher's prior consent, in any form of binding or
cover other than that in which it is published.

CONTENTS

The Mahindra & Mahindra Group — ix

Anand Mahindra: The Person — xv

Introduction — xxi

1. Develop the Courage to Follow Your Convictions — 1
2. Humility is More than a Virtue — 12
3. Focus on Frugal Innovation — 20
4. Only the Paranoid Survive — 34
5. Be Ruthlessly Competitive — 45
6. Empower Your Team with Freedom & Support — 50
7. Nurture Future Managers — 64
8. Stay Attuned to Your Networks, Competencies & Risks — 70
9. Choose Your Battles Carefully — 80

10 Hone Your Listening Skills	88
11 Homework Precedes Decisions	97
12 Grow by Acquisition	102
13 Invest with an Eye on the Future	116
14 Create One Identity	125
15 Joint Ventures Never Go Out of Style	130
16 The Scorpio Story	137
17 Summing Up: Management Lessons for Your Business	144

My father thought the world would be the same.
My children, however, wake up every day thinking the world will be different.
Let's begin emulating our children.
(It's) time to wake up and make the world different.

Mr Anand Mahindra, speaking at the
NASSCOM Leadership Summit, 2012[1]

---

[1] Kunal N. Talgeri, 'Inside the Merger!' *Fortune India*, December 5, 2012, last accessed February 18, 2019. https://www.fortuneindia.com/technology/inside-the-merger/100760; NASSCOM: National Association of Software and Services Companies

THE MAHINDRA & MAHINDRA GROUP

The fascinating story of Mahindra & Mahindra (M&M) begins with two brothers from Ludhiana in Punjab, India—Jagdish Chandra Mahindra and Kailash Chandra Mahindra. Jagdish, the eldest of nine children and grandfather of Mr Anand Mahindra, grew up to be India's first 'Iron & Steel Controller'—a position awarded to him by the Government of India during the Second World War. He was responsible for importing iron and steel to India. Kailash, his younger brother, was the Chairman of the Coal Commission. Eventually, the two brothers decided to launch an independent steel business. They sold their house in Kolkata (then Calcutta) to raise funds for their dream initiative. In 1945, together with Malik Ghulam Mohammed, one of the founders of the company, the Mahindra brothers set up a steel trading company in Ludhiana. It was called Mahindra and Mohammed.

During the Partition, Malik Ghulam Mohammed emigrated to Pakistan and became Pakistan's first finance minister. The company was renamed to its present name—

Mahindra & Mahindra. The two brothers shifted to Mumbai (then Bombay) and enthusiastically began running things at the helm.

M&M met with remarkable early success. It wasn't, however, as much beginner's luck as it was the complementary skill set of the two brothers. While Jagdish was the visionary and thought leader, Kailash was the execution expert. It was a winning team, and the results started to show within a few years.

In 1947, M&M started manufacturing the Willys Jeep in India, under licence from Willys-Overland Motors, an American company.[1] Soon, M&M became the leading Jeep manufacturer in India. The brothers, well attuned to the changing environment in India at the time, sensed the desire for globalization. In the 1950s and '60s, they decided to move to other segments like light commercial vehicles (LCVs) and agricultural tractors through tie-ups with foreign companies like Chrysler, Dr Beck, and International Harvester.

The early economic and political environment that M&M was exposed to, indirectly played a significant role in its growth. In the 1960s, India was a closed economy. M&M operated in

---

[1] MG Arun, 'Mahindra and Mahindra: Driving the change in India's automotive industry', *India Today*, August 11, 2017, accessed November 10, 2018. https://www.indiatoday.in/magazine/cover-story/story/20170821-mahindra-mahindra-car-company-anand-mahindra-automotive-industry-muv-suv-segment-1028902-2017-08-11;
Kushan Mitra, 'We will create a system that is impregnable', *Business Today*, September 13, 2011, accessed November 8, 2018, https://www.businesstoday.in/opinion/interviews/anand-mahindra-satyam-rise/story/18639.html

an environment with hardly any competition. The company faced negligible pressure to develop or import new technology, since they were the only major player in their segment. In that restrictive atmosphere, where the government tightly controlled industrial capacities, there was only one approach that the group could take for expansion: diversification into unrelated sectors. Slowly but steadily, M&M expanded into industries like oil-rig leasing, instrumentation, chemicals, fibreglass, and nuclear power.[2] It was a silent growth strategy that would see the group transform into a juggernaut to be reckoned with.

Subsequently in the 1990s, with liberalization unleashed in India, M&M moved from growth by diversification, to experimenting with a market-led growth approach by seeking to enter newer markets, primarily through takeovers and acquisitions. In 2008, the group entered the two-wheeler segment by taking over Kinetic Motors, Honda's former Indian partner.[3] Soon after this, M&M solidified its presence in the sector with another acquisition—that of a 51 per cent stake in Peugeot Motocycles, a French scooters and small motorcycles manufacturer.

---

[2] Pavan Lall, 'Anand Mahindra, adventure capitalist', *Fortune India*, December 5, 2010. Accessed November 11, 2018. https://www.fortuneindia.com/people/anand-mahindra-adventure-capitalist/101132

[3] Muntaser Mirkar, 'Mahindra acquires 80% in Kinetic Motor Cycles', *The Economic Times*, August 7, 2008, accessed March 2, 2019 https://economictimes.indiatimes.com/auto/mahindra-acquires-80-in-kinetic-motor-cycles/articleshow/3335578.cms?from=mdr

The year 2011 was an especially significant year for the group, with M&M purchasing the Indian Reva Electric Car company as well as entering the micro drip irrigation sector with the takeover of EPC Industries in Nashik. The company closed the year with a bang: the purchase of a 76.06 per cent stake in Pininfarina S.p.A, an Italian car design company, for ₹25.3 million (around ₹186.7 crore) in December. The deal was solemnized with Tech Mahindra Ltd, an affiliate of the M&M Group.

In 2015, M&M acquired SsangYong Motor Company, a Korean automobile company.[4] M&M now looked towards foreign markets, aiming to mark its entry into overseas territories. In January 2017, it entered the industrial landscape of Turkey with the acquisition of a 75.1 per cent equity stake in Hisarlar (Hisarlar Makina Sanayi Ve Ticaret Anonim Şirketi), a farm equipment company. Later that year, in September, the group also took over Erkunt Traktor Sanayii A.Ş., a Turkish tractor manufacturer, for a whopping ₹800 crore.

Today, the M&M Group is a $20.7 billion company, with a presence in over hundred countries across the globe, employing more than 2,40,000 people. It is a company that started with its eye on vehicles but has since developed deep-rooted interests and pursuits spanning aerospace, auto components, defence, financial services, information technology (IT) and hospitality.

---

[4]NDTV Auto Team, 'Mahindra Two Wheelers Acquires 51% Stake in Peugeot Motocycles', NDTV Auto, January 20, 2015, accessed March 2, 2019 https://auto.ndtv.com/news/mahindra-two-wheelers-acquires-51-stake-in-peugeot-motocycles-729912

If the realm of industries that M&M interests itself in seems daunting, there is one vital observation to make: it has ensured that its expansion has been rapid but not superficial. In the seventy-four years that have gone by since the group's inception, M&M has developed businesses that have emerged as leaders in the industries in which they operate. As of 2019, M&M is the world's largest tractor manufacturer by volume, the largest multi-brand pre-owned car company, and the largest rural Non Banking Financial Company (NBFC) in India. It is also one of India's largest vacation suppliers and among the top five IT service providers in the country.

ANAND MAHINDRA: THE PERSON

For Mr Anand Mahindra, a flair for business could well be in his genes. He is the son of Mr Harish Mahindra, the late industrialist who was the founding chairman of the Mahindra Ugine Steel Company (MUSCO), and Mrs Indira Mahindra. His uncle, Mr Keshub Mahindra, served as the Chairman of the M&M Group for over forty-five years, expanding the business across sectors and forging meaningful alliances.

Born on 1 May 1955[1], Mr Anand Mahindra went on to study at the Lawrence School, Lovedale, Ooty.[2] After completing his schooling, he pursued architecture from the JJ College of Architecture in Mumbai. Surprisingly, Mr Mahindra also holds a bachelor's degree in Film Studies from Harvard University; he pursued this educational

---

[1]https://en.wikipedia.org/wiki/Anand_Mahindra, accessed March 11, 2019.
[2]https://economictimes.indiatimes.com/magazines/panache/kabaddi-deserves-a-league-of-its-own-anand-mahindra/articleshow/33536965.cms, accessed March 11, 2019.

programme under the esteemed university's Department of Visual and Environmental Studies.[3] He subsequently received a master's degree in Business Administration (MBA) from the Harvard Business School, pursuing the course from 1979 to 1981.

After receiving his MBA in 1981, Mr Mahindra joined MUSCO as the executive assistant to the finance director. In 1989, he was appointed the president and deputy managing director (MD) of MUSCO. On 4 April 1991, he rose to the position of deputy MD of the M&M Group. His personal and professional growth from there on was meteoric. In April 1997, Mr Mahindra was elected the MD of M&M. Soon after, in 2001, he was appointed the vice chairman. In August 2012, after the retirement of his uncle, Mr Keshub Mahindra, he took over the reins as the MD and chairman of the M&M Group. His official designation underwent a slight modification in November 2016, when he assumed the position of executive chairman of M&M while continuing to be at the helm of affairs as the Group chairman.[4]

With time, Mr Anand Mahindra has established a steady reputation as a capable and dependable leader. His exceptional leadership abilities are, in fact, internationally acknowledged. In 2008, the Harvard Business School called him the 'Renaissance Man' while awarding him the Alumni

---

[3] https://www.linkedin.com/in/anand-mahindra-a5959798/, accessed March 11, 2019.
[4] https://en.wikipedia.org/wiki/Anand_Mahindra, accessed March 11, 2019.

Achievement Award.[5] In 2014, the *Fortune* magazine ranked him amongst the world's '50 Great Leaders', stating[6]:

> In an era that feels starved for leadership, we've found men and women who will inspire you—some famous, others little known, all of them energizing their followers and making the world better. A third-generation corporate aristocrat, Mr Mahindra has aggressively expanded the big conglomerate through acquisitions in autos, computer services, aeronautics, and more, while maintaining the company's standing as one of India's most sought-after employers. The company remains well regarded in Indian society as he has reinforced a policy of integrity in a notoriously corrupt environment.

The editor's note for Mr Mahindra aptly captured the essence of the man—a low-key leader who has nonetheless made a tremendous impact on the business environment in India.

---

[5]https://www.alumni.hbs.edu/stories/Pages/story-bulletin.aspx?num=1994, accessed March 11, 2019
Pavan Lall, 'Anand Mahindra, adventure capitalist', *Fortune India*, December 5, 2010, accessed November 11, 2018. https://www.fortuneindia.com/people/anand-mahindra-adventure-capitalist/101132
[6]Fortune Editors, The World's 50 Greatest Leaders (2014) March 20, 2014, accessed November 8, 2018. http://fortune.com/2014/03/20/worlds-50-greatest-leaders/

TAPPING THE POWER OF SOCIAL MEDIA

In April 2009, Mr Anand Mahindra started posting updates on Twitter. As of 2019, his Twitter account has 6.93 million followers and over 18,300 tweets.[7] His tweets cover a wide range of subjects related not only to M&M but also to contemporary topics like sports, physical fitness and women's empowerment. In an interview in 2014 with *The Economic Times*, he stated that social media is not a pastime but one of the most underutilized, though critical, tools for survival in the digital era, for today's Chief Executive Officer (CEOs).[8]

Not content with using the popular social media platform as a unidirectional channel, Mr Mahindra often responds to comments made by others. He is, perhaps, one of the very few Indian industrialists who have effectively used Twitter to reach out to large groups of people and capture the pulse of a global audience. The M&M leader is among a handful of notable CEOs in India who have started using Twitter. Others include Mr Harsh Goenka, Chairman, RPG Group and

---

[7] https://twitter.com/anandmahindra, accessed November 11, 2018
[8] Lijee Philip, 'Social Media is a critical tool for survival in the digital era: Anand Mahindra, M&M.' *The Economic Times*, June 4, 2014, accessed March 11, 2019, https://economictimes.indiatimes.com/industry/social-media-is-a-critical-tool-for-survival-in-the-digital-era-anand-mahindra-mm/articleshow/36029946.cms
Pavan Lall, 'Anand Mahindra, adventure capitalist', *Fortune India*, December 5, 2010, accessed November 11, 2018. https://www.fortuneindia.com/people/anand-mahindra-adventure-capitalist/101132

Anand Mahindra: The Person

Mr Nandan Nilekani, Non-executive Chairman, Infosys. However, Mr Mahindra's present follower base (as of 2018) is larger than that of most of his contemporaries.

A LEADER WHO LEADS WITH ACTIONS

Mr Anand Mahindra has consistently maintained a low profile, choosing to let his actions speak louder than his words. He adopts a relatively frugal lifestyle, driving his own car—a Scorpio. As the group executive chairman, he draws a considerably lower compensation (₹8.03 crore) compared to that drawn by Mr Pawan Goenka, the Group MD (₹12.21 crore). As per the group's annual report (2017–18), Mr Mahindra's compensation stood at ₹8.7 crore, excluding the perquisite value of Employee Stock Option Plans (ESOPs) exercised.[9] This difference is noteworthy, as it shows how Mr Mahindra has no qualms about letting other members of his business earn more than him. This is a monumental sign of a professionally managed company, raising loyalties as well as cementing employee commitment.

In his day-to-day life, Mr Anand Mahindra is regarded as a good listener. Many members on the board of the M&M Group, as well as other boards on which Mr Mahindra

---

[9] PTI, 'Mahindra MD Pawan Goenka's remuneration grew 65% in FY18', *The Economic Times*, July 23, 2018, accessed November 11, 2018. https://economictimes.indiatimes.com/news/company/corporate-trends/mahindra-md-pawan-goenkas-remuneration-grew-65-in-fy18/articleshow/65107936.cms

is a member, describe him as someone with exceptional clarity of thought. They observe that he patiently listens to all the members of his team and seeks out conversations from everyone: from his customers to his contemporaries at the annual World Economic Forum in Davos; and from his employees to experts and peers from Harvard Business School. Committed to the overall professional development of his personnel, he takes his team members and their spouses to an executive development programme to Harvard Business School in May every year.

INTRODUCTION

For any business house to flourish, the single most important ingredient is a clear vision. In his running of the M&M Group, Mr Anand Mahindra has adopted a view he believes in, and he has unflinchingly adhered to it. In an interview with Pavan Lall in *Fortune India*, Mr Mahindra described his job as 'the business of entrepreneurship'. He said, 'Down the road we became enlightened venture capitalists and then aggressive private equity players'.[1]

ADOPTING THE PRIVATE EQUITY APPROACH

Steering the business as if it were a private equity firm has been the mainstay of Mr Anand Mahindra as the chairman of

---

[1] Pavan Lall, 'Anand Mahindra, adventure capitalist', *Fortune India*, December 5, 2010, accessed November 11, 2018. https://www.fortuneindia.com/people/anand-mahindra-adventure-capitalist/101132

the M&M Group. Years down the line, he continues to play the role of a private equity investor, defining his company as a 'utility and automobile company' that has a portfolio of investments. He firmly believes that business families should always behave like aggressive private equity companies that 'allocate capital, demand performance, create synergies, sustain value systems and implement good governance practices'.[2]

Expanding on the private equity approach for running his business, Mr Mahindra also recommends letting professional managers look after the daily operations of the companies. In an interview with *Outlook Business*, where he discussed the famous revamp of the M&M Group in 1994, Mr Mahindra said: 'I provided managerial focus to all our businesses. Dedicated teams of managers have run our businesses since then. I kicked myself upstairs to make sure the structure would work; otherwise, I'd be breathing down the presidents' necks every day, defeating the idea of managerial focus.'[3]

True to his words, Mr Anand Mahindra has consistently treated his business as a federation, not a conglomerate. How are the two different? A **conglomerate** is a huge company with

---

[2] Thomas A. Stewart and Anand P. Raman, 'Finding a Higher Gear,' *Harvard Business Review*, July-August 2008, accessed April 10, 2019. https://hbr.org/2008/07/finding-a-higher-gear

[3] V. Keshavdev, 'The Boss Anand Mahindra', *Outlook Business*, July 10, 2015, accessed November 2018. https://www.outlookbusiness.com/specials/the-boss-anand-mahindra-1258

divisions performing various businesses. The stock market values the company as the sum of those divisions. On the other hand, a **federation** is a group of independent companies with each company focused on one area. The owner binds these companies together, effectively unifying them into one functional whole. The M&M Group acts as a federation where managers are empowered to look after the running of various businesses, with limited day-to-day interference seeping down from the top. But all the independent businesses have the steady and reassuring support of the leader, egging them on to add value to the overall group. We discuss this in further detail in Chapter 8.

SMART ACQUISITIONS AND CAREFUL DIVERSIFICATION

Acquisitions have played a significant role in the growth trajectory of Mr Anand Mahindra and his business empire.[4] He has, with time and experience, developed a keen business acumen for handpicking companies with growth potential and choosing to buy them out to fuel business growth. In making these acquisitions, Mr Mahindra has carved a unique path—frequently going against popular opinion or the scepticism shown by market observers. Till date, Mr Mahindra has bought over twenty companies for various valuations, ranging

---

[4]Pavan Lall, 'Anand Mahindra, adventure capitalist', *Fortune India*, December 5, 2010, accessed November 11, 2018. https://www.fortuneindia.com/people/anand-mahindra-adventure-capitalist/101132

from ₹3 crore for iPolicy Networks to ₹1,408 crore for Punjab Tractors.[5]

Though Mr Anand Mahindra has bought over many companies, he has also played the part of an angel investor in start-ups where the buyout option did not seem worthwhile. In 2007, for instance, he started Mahindra Odyssea to build powerboats. This decision emanated from his conviction and observation of the rising incomes in India, which he expected would increase the demand for powerboats. Some of Mr Mahindra's decisions may seem like speculative bets to anyone watching from the sidelines, but if one were to take a closer look, they would realize that these are the outcomes of carefully applied thought, which is based on his vision of partnering in projects that are likely to pay off in the future.

While making business decisions, Mr Anand Mahindra has relied on a variety of strategies. He has neither stayed limited to the safe comfort zone of being in only one industry, nor has he gambled big on expensive acquisitions. One approach that has held him in good stead throughout his experimentation with his business models, is a steady hand on organizational structure. Soon after taking over as the chairman, Mr Mahindra organized the group into six sectors: automotive, automotive components, farm equipment, financial services, infrastructure and software. As of 2018, the M&M Group is

---

[5]Pavan Lall, 'Anand Mahindra, adventure capitalist', *Fortune India*, December 5, 2010, accessed November 11, 2018. https://www.fortuneindia.com/people/anand-mahindra-adventure-capitalist/101132

present in eleven sectors: aerospace and defence, aftermarket, agri-business, automotive, farm equipment, financial services, hospitality, IT, partners, real estate and two-wheelers.

The industry-wise presence of the group is even more overwhelming. The group operates in twenty-two industries including aerospace, aftermarket, clean energy, construction equipment, consulting, defence, hospitality, insurance broking, logistics, power back-up, real estate and infrastructure, retail, rural housing finance, and steel and equipment finance. In many of these businesses, the group has established itself as the frontrunner. The M&M Group is now India's largest utility vehicle maker, India's largest NBFC in the rural and semi-rural sectors, and the topmost multi-brand-certified, used-car company in the country. It is also among India's top three third-party logistics service providers and one of the top five IT service providers.

This impressive presence across a wide spectrum of industry sectors hasn't been just plain luck or by accident; it is the outcome of a well-thought-out and meticulously implemented diversification strategy. Mr Anand Mahindra has diversified into sectors where he perceived opportunities and future potential, just like the rule he follows while making acquisitions.

His keen focus on creating value and ensuring growth has helped the M&M Group diversify into fast-growing areas. From a business house that concentrated on automotive and farm equipment, Mr Mahindra has transformed M&M into a group that has significant investments in hospitality, defence, information technology, and electric vehicles. The M&M Group has risen from its traditional strengths of auto manufacturing to meaningful returns on investments in allied sectors. In 2018, only 55 per cent of the group's turnover came from the automobile and farm equipment sector. As of today, the auto segment comprises less than 50 per cent of the group's capitalization. The payouts from the overseas acquisitions were tangible too, with over 49 per cent of the group's turnover coming from outside India as of FY18.[6]

Mr Anand Mahindra has applied his mantra of seeking potential in framing the group's exit strategies as well. This encouraged him to steer his group's exit from the sectors of oil drilling and instrumentation, which were not proving to be lucrative for the business. Unwilling to let enthusiasm overrule business logic, Mr Mahindra has also adopted a conservative approach towards cash-intensive industries like telecom and retail.

This book takes a close look at the journey of Mr Anand Mahindra. It traces the growth trajectory of the M&M Group from its initial days to the mega business empire it has become today. In the course of this mesmerising journey, we will seek to learn essential management lessons from this renowned but low-key industrialist. These should be of immense use for entrepreneurs, business owners, and also anyone with a passion for adding value to the economic biosphere.

---

[6]Mahindra Group Presentation on Company Website, https://www.mahindra.com/resources/pdf/about-us/mahindra-rise-brochure-oct-2018.pdf, accessed March 12, 2019.

1
DEVELOP THE COURAGE TO FOLLOW YOUR CONVICTIONS

CONSULT THOSE YOU TRUST, BUT MAKE YOUR DECISIONS BASED ON PERSONAL ASSESSMENT AND CONVICTION

Right from the outset, Mr Anand Mahindra has adopted a highly personal style of decision-making. While taking important and sensitive decisions for his business, he prefers to consult several people, including his professional teams and other stakeholders of M&M. However, the ultimate decision is almost invariably based on his assessment of what would make his companies successful, even if it is contrary to what the common thought is. His approach demonstrates the courage of being unafraid to go off the beaten path, where few have trodden before.

One may ask how Mr Mahindra garners the courage to adopt the path less taken, even when a wrong move could mean a potential risk for the business. To an extent, it is possible that his background in the Humanities and years spent studying film-making at Harvard, even though he always had a flair for science, influenced his outlook towards life. This diverse background may have influenced his decision-making process in the role that he subsequently took as the head of a business.

Another situational factor that has steeled Mr Mahindra's resolve and courage to experiment is the abundance of challenges. Even in the early days, when he hadn't yet settled down into his new job, unforeseen problems lurked all around the M&M Group. For this business leader, the path to growth hasn't been smooth; in fact, it has been littered with multiple battles. But challenges in all shapes and sizes—many of them unexpected—have played a monumental role in strengthening Mr Mahindra's conviction in his decisions.

EXPANDING MUSCO

After receiving his bachelor's degree in the film studies programme of the Department of Visual and Environmental Studies[1] of Harvard University, Mr Anand Mahindra was initially considering going into the movie business. However, he eventually decided to go to Harvard Business School. In 1981, he joined his father at MUSCO. Upon joining, his first major responsibility was to restructure and diversify MUSCO.

---

[1] https://alumni.harvard.edu/stories/anand-mahindra-77-mba-81-gives-harvard-10-million-for-humanities-center, accessed March 12, 2019

At the time of Mr Mahindra's joining, MUSCO possessed the licence to manufacture alloys and specialized steel products using electric arc furnaces. It was a six-player industry and the competition was not too severe. But shortly after Mr Mahindra assumed his position as the executive assistant, the Government of India did something that proved to be a game changer. It decided to issue licences to thirty new producers in the arc furnace industry, thereby allowing them to import state-of-the-art technology and set up small but efficient steel plants in India.[2] This expanded the size of the entire industry to almost six times that of the earlier size![3]

At MUSCO, a crisis meeting was organized to understand the implications of the announcement. During his conversations with the various managers in the company, Mr Anand Mahindra became aware of a huge roadblock. In light of the expanding industry size and rising competition, it was imperative for MUSCO to optimize their costs. However, the managers were unfamiliar with the very concept of cost curves (for example, how do costs behave) or how to maximize contribution by lowering prices.

Undaunted by the less-than-ideal atmosphere, Mr Mahindra applied his management learning to streamline

---

[2] Thomas Stewart and Anand Raman, 'Finding a Higher Gear', *Harvard Business Review*, July-August 2008, accessed November 2018. https://hbr.org/2008/07/finding-a-higher-gear

[3] V. Keshavdev, 'The Boss Anand Mahindra', *Outlook Business*, July 10, 2015, accessed November 2018. https://www.outlookbusiness.com/specials/the-boss/anand-mahindra-1258

the supply chain. He also cleared up the inventory. Slowly but steadily, his actions effected the turnaround of MUSCO. In 1989, he was appointed the president and deputy MD of the company. This stint turned out to be the mega preparation for his eventual leadership role at M&M, which he joined in 1991.

THE CRUCIBLE TEST

Mr Anand Mahindra joined M&M as its deputy MD. He started with the factory shop floor, focusing on labour relations and research and development (R&D). He chose to understand the working of the group from the grass-root level, instead of sitting at the corporate office. The latter, perhaps, would have limited the depth of his judgements. Little could he have known that a massive challenge lurking in the corner would hit him with full fury in the very first year of his joining! The crisis came from unexpected quarters and almost threatened his life.

Earlier, in the 1980s, the world had gone through an oil crisis during the time of the Iran-Iraq war. The demand for vehicles fell sharply, severely hitting the revenues of the M&M Group. The Government of India imposed a 66 per cent excise duty on jeeps, almost driving the proverbial last nail into the coffin. The situation steadily worsened.

In 1991, the M&M Group was busy manufacturing tractors and jeeps. According to the norms of the Indian economy at the time, the automobile sector was permitted 100 per cent foreign investment. This was a huge pain point for M&M primarily because they manufactured these two products (tractors and jeeps) quite inefficiently. The labour force worked in conditions of extremely low productivity.[4] Mr Bharat Doshi, the executive director and group chief financial officer (CFO) at the time, recalled in an interview[5] that in 1992–93, M&M manufactured 35,000 tractors and 38,000 vehicles with a labour force of 17,000. Maruti, on the other hand, produced 1,22,000 vehicles with 4,000 people. That was almost double the output with a quarter of the workforce!

It was this background and the impending threat to their existence that bothered Mr Anand Mahindra. By July 1991, Mr Mahindra decided that this situation of insanely poor productivity could not be allowed to continue. If fixing the situation required tough and possibly unpopular decisions, so be it. As the calendar year veered close to Diwali, one of the biggest Hindu festivals in India, Mr Anand Mahindra made a shocking announcement.

The Diwali bonuses that year would be linked to productivity. The workers should be informed that there would be no Diwali bonus unless they managed to step up productivity.

---

[4]Kushan Mitra, 'Top Gun,' *Business Today*, October 2, 2011, accessed October 10, 2018. https://www.businesstoday.in/magazine/cover-story/anand-mahindra-mandm-company-acquisitions/story/18656.html

[5]V. Keshavdev, 'The Boss Anand Mahindra', *Outlook Business*, July 10, 2015, accessed November 2018. https://www.outlookbusiness.com/specials/the-boss-anand-mahindra-1258

Not surprisingly, this decision was met with massive resistance in the factories. The workers in the Kandivali factory of Mumbai went on strike, protesting against this 'unfair' announcement. Large groups of agitated workers became increasingly upset against the management for this decision. When Mr Mahindra visited the Kandivali office with some of his senior executives, the workers surrounded him in a gherao, refusing to let him leave the spot. This was a situation that could become ugly and discourage even the most spirited of business leaders. But Mr Mahindra refused to budge from the stand that he had taken.

Eventually, many long and tense hours after the agitation, the workers came around and agreed to the clause of Diwali bonuses being linked to increased productivity. The 1,230 labourers at the M&M engine plant at Igatpuri, Maharashtra, who had firmly decided not to produce more than seventy engines per day, also agreed to the condition. Over the next three years, the productivity gains in M&M went up by almost 150 per cent.[6]

Perhaps, the early challenge that Mr Anand Mahindra faced at M&M, and the subsequent steps he took to raise the productivity, proved to be a blessing in disguise. They helped the company stay relevant even in the face of stiffening competition, especially in 1997 when Toyota, a Japanese

---

[6]Kushan Mitra, 'Top Gun,' *Business Today*, October 2, 2011, accessed October 10, 2018. https://www.businesstoday.in/magazine/cover-story/anand-mahindra-mandm-company-acquisitions/story/18656.html

multinational automotive manufacturer, and many other multinational companies entered India. By then, Mr Mahindra had taken over as the MD of M&M, and his initial exposure to the volatile environment helped him get a head start on the then fiercely competitive Indian auto sector.

THE AUTOMOTIVE DECISION

In the early 1990s, the M&M Group hired McKinsey & Company, the globally renowned management consulting company, to advise them on the future of their business. McKinsey & Company, after doing their groundwork, came up with a detailed report with their strong and maybe tough suggestion for the future of M&M.[7] The report recommended that the group divest its automotive business, as it was too small, and focus instead on the tractor business. M&M would not, the report stated, be able to compete against the mammoth players that had entered the auto sector. This was the post-liberalization era, so there was a huge increase in foreign collaborations, joint ventures (JVs) and international players setting up shop or desiring to do so, in India.

Mr Anand Mahindra was unsettled by this report. While he recognized the changing dynamics in the auto sector, he was against making an exit. He discussed the proposal with the M&M board. Most of the members of the board felt

---

[7] V. Keshavdev, 'The Boss Anand Mahindra', *Outlook Business*, July 10, 2015, accessed November 2018. https://www.outlookbusiness.com/specials/the-boss-anand-mahindra-1258

that the recommendation made by the consultants should be seriously considered. But, at the same time, the board suggested that they also assess the opinion of the automotive team. Not surprisingly, the automotive team was against the recommendation. The decision went into limbo, causing the automotive business of the group to lose valuable time. Mr Mahindra decided to take quick action to avert further delays due to slow decision-making. In 1993, the M&M Group tied up with Ford, a multinational automaker headquartered in Detroit, to manufacture the Escort—a sedan—in India.[8] It was a decision that, as we shall see in later chapters, had deep implications for the future of the group.

Amidst the transforming economic environment in India, Mr Mahindra always had the conviction that his group could take on the big, global players on the same terms. In 1994, only three years after he assumed the role of the deputy MD of M&M, he unleashed a full-blown strategy for globalization and diversification within the company, steering his group into the ranks of the top global firms of the time.

LONG-TERM OBJECTIVES REQUIRE RISK-TAKING

As a businessman, Mr Anand Mahindra epitomises the importance of the two most important tools for a leader: personal conviction and determination.

---

[8]V. Keshavdev, 'The Boss Anand Mahindra', *Outlook Business*, July 10, 2015, accessed November 2018. https://www.outlookbusiness.com/specials/the-boss/anand-mahindra-1258

Even when he was just starting off as a leader, Mr Mahindra did not hesitate to take a tough stand towards the labour force. This was a monumental risk not only for his company but also for his personal safety and credibility. He risked what could have been a long period of labour strikes or labour unrest—situations that have brought on the dismal end of many organizations.

In taking this bold step, he trusted his assessment of the changing business environment that mandated transforming the way things worked in his company. The Indian market had opened up to foreign players who were not only competitive but also much more productive. The JV of Maruti-Suzuki had already achieved a significantly higher rate of efficiency and productivity as compared to M&M, and this would have a telling impact on the long-term performance and even the subsequent survival of the group. Mr Mahindra understood this precarious situation and its seriousness, which probably led to his insistence of demanding higher productivity. While the move had a short-term negative impact—a consequence that could have easily become uglier—it effected brilliant long-term results. In fact, this step was the deciding move that improved the fortunes of the company within a very short span of three years from 1991.

Was it foolhardy to put his life at risk? Why didn't Mr Anand Mahindra delegate this task of communicating with the labour force and coming up with a strategy to improve overall productivity, to his management team? His managers were a group of capable professionals and exclusively trained to arrive at such decisions. A leader's willingness to assume centrestage in taking difficult decisions, without being afraid of losing face or popularity, demonstrates a high degree of commitment and professionalism. It takes strength to risk being openly criticized by stakeholders and covertly loathed by employees.

There is a school of thought, which was stated in a *Harvard Business Review* article,[9] which mentions that true leaders have faced adversity, and these adversarial experiences have shaped their lives. These leaders have learnt from such experiences to emerge stronger and wiser. And this is a determining characteristic of most well-known leaders. Similarly, Mr Mahindra has spoken constantly about taking on newer responsibilities and facing adversarial conditions, and these have played a very significant role in preparing him for the challenges that lay ahead. This is an important factor for training future managers. It is jokingly said that Indian businessmen are so accustomed to facing challenges in very tough environments, that they can't excel in environments where they are allowed to work and are left alone!

To sum up, Mr Anand Mahindra exemplifies that sticking to one's convictions in business is easier said than done. It is easy to make tall promises. Everyone wants to be popular and be the object of praise and paeans of glory. When consultants and other key persons around you have

---

[9] Warren G. Bennis and Robert J. Thomas, 'Crucibles of Leadership', *Harvard Business Review*, September, 2002.

thoughts that are contrary to your own, naysayers may claim that your beliefs are fraught with risks. Decision-making in such circumstances can become tricky. True leaders are those, who can take tough calls that are necessary for the long-term success of the business. They have the courage to carry out their convictions and adhere to their vision to achieve success. You can call it being courageous or overconfident; I leave it to you to decide for yourself. But history has shown that most successful companies have succeeded only because they had leaders who did not hesitate to make such choices.

2

HUMILITY IS MORE THAN A VIRTUE

BE A HUMBLE LEADER, FOR IT WILL WIN YOU SUPPORT FROM YOUR PEOPLE AND EMPOWER YOU WITH THE STRENGTH TO EXECUTE YOUR PLANS

In modern times, it seems most fashionable to claim that a business leader at the top is as humble as a working-class man. Unfortunately, this purported humility is rarely deep-seated but generally superficial, intended to become fodder for public relations machinery to extensively be covered across various media. With Mr Anand Mahindra, on the contrary, humility is not only a virtue, but also a trait ingrained in all his business dealings.

People who work with Mr Mahindra at M&M claim that he is a humble leader whose position does not overshadow his genuine concern for his team members. Mr Bharat Doshi, the executive director and Group CFO from 1992 to 2013, remembers him from when he first joined the group as the deputy MD. He was a keen young man, recollects Mr Doshi, who was eager to learn and didn't possess even a shred of self-entitlement. He also recalls that Mr Mahindra was always observant, enthusiastic about asking questions, and interested in perceiving everything with a fresh set of eyes, instead of silently agreeing with everything he was told.[10]

Why does Mr Mahindra make a statement with his humility? The answer is straightforward: it is a win-win situation both for personal growth and business gains. Mr Mahindra prioritizes the growth of his people so they can be empowered to solve the problems at hand. His humility helps him become a partner and facilitator in problem-solving, wherein he applies his knowledge and experience to help his people emerge triumphant in challenging business scenarios. How can a haughty leader who finds it beneath himself to listen and learn from his employees, ever achieve quick business solutions?

Mr Anand Mahindra's humility has also paid rich dividends in cementing his belief in his products and establishing a company-wide culture of ownership. He propagates the concept of being grounded to accept business realities for what they are and never perceiving any team member too insignificant to be consulted for advice.

---

[10] V. Keshavdev, 'The Boss Anand Mahindra', *Outlook Business*, July 10, 2015, accessed November 2018. https://www.outlookbusiness.com/specials/the-boss/anand-mahindra-1258

'DRIVING' THE CHANGE

Before joining Harvard Business School to pursue his MBA, Mr Anand Mahindra spent a year working at the group and learning the ropes. He worked in different locations, travelling from one office to another. Mr Bharat Doshi recalled that Mr Mahindra, just like the rest of the executives of the group, travelled to Kandivali by train when he could have easily chosen to travel by car.[11]

When Mr Mahindra started travelling by car, he preferred driving himself to work, choosing not to avail the services of a chauffeur. Mr Mahindra usually drives cars that are produced by M&M. He is quite a car aficionado and takes pride in driving the newest vehicles to get a first-hand experience of what they offer. He tweets about his latest vehicle acquisitions too, with the most recent one being the Alturas G4.[12] On his Twitter page, he wrote: 'Finally took delivery of my Alturas G4. I named my TUV 3OO [sic] plus the 'Grey Ghost.' Need a name for this new beautiful beast. All ideas welcome. The person who suggests the chosen name will get 2 Mahindra die cast scale models (Not the Alturas scale model—that's not ready yet!)'

---

[11] V. Keshavdev, 'The Boss Anand Mahindra', *Outlook Business*, July 10, 2015, accessed November 2018. https://www.outlookbusiness.com/specials/the-boss/anand-mahindra-1258

[12] Anwesha Madhukalya, 'Anand Mahindra throws open challenge to name his new car; winner to get a prize', *Business Today*, January 16, 2019, accessed February 17, 2019, https://www.businesstoday.in/sectors/auto/anand-mahindra-throws-open-challenge-name-new-car-winner-get-prize/story/310598.html

The Battista, when launched in Geneva on 4 March 2019 was stated to be the world's first luxury electric hyper-performance grand tourer and the first solely Pininfarina-badged car.[13] Pininfarina had been a design studio, designing for some of the best-known car manufacturers globally, but had never launched a car under its own name. Mr Mahindra's sense of humour was apparent when a Twitter follower asked him, '*Sir, kitna deti hai?*' (Sir, how much does it give?) in an apparent reference to the fuel economy of the car. Mr Mahindra's prompt reply was, '*Sirji, electric hai...Shock deti hai!*' (Sir, it is an electric vehicle... It gives electric shocks!).[14]

His tendency to drive himself to work and engage in conversation with his people come together beautifully to build a healthy working environment in his organization. His use of social media has also played a constructive role in furthering this. In January 2019, he invited his followers to send in suggestions to christen his new car; his old car, as he stated in the tweet above, was called the 'Grey Ghost'. Today, when the Indian auto marketplace abounds in vehicles, Mr Mahindra's office sees a vast assortment of cars. But even though his employees may use cars made by other

---

[13]https://www.mahindra.com/news-room/press-release/pininifarina-battista-the-world-s-first-pure-electric-luxury-hyper-gt-revealed, accessed March 12, 2019

[14]Rishabh Jain, 'Pininfarina Battista kitna deti hain - Anand Mahindra replies to twitter user,' Rushlane online, March 10, 2019, accessed March 12, 2019. https://www.rushlane.com/pininfarina-battista-kitna-deti-hain-12300285.html

manufacturers, he drives only a Mahindra-manufactured vehicle.

THE TATA-MAHINDRA EQUATION

In 2012, the auto sector in India was witness to an incident that startled many. M&M had not only challenged Tata Motors, the long-established market champion in the passenger cars and vehicles segment, but had also overtaken it to occupy the third position. Tata Motors had retained its top spot in Indian commercial vehicles, where it was still the market leader, but the overtake was a panic-inducing moment for the Tata Group.

Addressing his shareholders at the Annual General Meeting of Tata Motors in 2012 in Mumbai, Ratan Tata expressed his grief at the situation. He admitted to being 'saddened' and 'ashamed' that Tata Motors had been thus overtaken by M&M, the homegrown rival. Mr Tata also said,[15]

> I have great respect for what Mahindra & Mahindra has been able to do. I also have a certain degree of sadness and shame that we have let that happen. So I hope the spirit of this company will ensure that we undertake

---

[15] PTI, Mumbai, 'Ratan Tata hails M&M, says sad that the company has overtaken Tata Motors,' *Business Today* online, August 11, 2012, accessed March 12, 2019, https://www.businesstoday.in/current/corporate/tata-motors-ratan-tata-hails-mahindra-and-mahindra/story/187102.html

every step to get back to the prominent position and not let a competitor do better than us, by being first in everything we do.

Although this was a triumphant moment for M&M, Mr Anand Mahindra did not choose to gloat. Instead, he let his humility win the day by opting to be gracious. On Twitter, he responded to Mr Tata's comments by saying that the fellow businessman had been extraordinarily humble and generous. Mr Mahindra further stated that the M&M Group took the development as 'a pat on the back from a big brother'—something that 'inspires us to work harder'.[16]

While many business leaders would have seized the moment to flood the papers with full-page advertisements and interviews proclaiming victory, Mr Mahindra decided to underplay the event and view it as a little laurel in the larger scheme of things.

EARN GOODWILL THROUGH MATURITY AND HUMILITY

Mr Anand Mahindra's humility demonstrates a commendable sense of work ethics and discipline. His eagerness to learn and tendency to probe not only endears him to his people but also helps him grasp the complexities of a situation faster. The act

---

[16]PTI News, New Delhi, 'Ratan Tata's comment a pat on the back from a big brother: Anand Mahindra,' *Business Today*, August 11, 2012. Accessed October 17, 2018. https://www.businesstoday.in/current/corporate/anand-mahindra-says-ratan-tatas-comment-a-pat-on-the-back/story/187103.html

of asking questions is like stating, 'I do not know this,' and this is a statement that many people, especially those in senior positions, find impossible to utter.

The incident of choosing to travel to the Kandivali factory by train and the decision not to employ a driver might seem trivial, but both instances showcase a deep-seated sense of responsibility. They also indicate the absence of a feeling of entitlement that many successors born into wealth are prone to exhibit.

It could be argued that the time that Mr Mahindra spends on mundane activities like driving and travelling by train could be more effectively utilized in value-added activities. Perhaps, yes. However, it is the humility driving his actions, which has been instrumental in helping him expand his business by leaps and bounds. It connects him to his people, to the tough ground realities and to the harsh market situations that may be otherwise ambiguous when seen from air-conditioned offices.

There is another subtle objective that Mr Anand Mahindra succeeds in achieving by driving cars manufactured by his own company: a public display of confidence in his products. The simple act of driving Mahindra-manufactured cars sends a powerful message to all his stakeholders and customers. It assures his audiences of the confidence and pride the chairman has in what the company produces. Imagine the message that would go out if the chairman (as also the other executives of the company) preferred products manufactured by competitors over their own. It would be, at best, a mixed message implying that the products might be passable but weren't good enough for the senior management to use.

Believing in and using one's products are simple strategies to build customer trust, which unfortunately, most companies overlook. It is also one of the simplest methods of receiving unbiased feedback. Think about how the members of the manufacturing division would stay on their toes if they knew that the top management would be driving the cars that they manufacture!

Here's the final takeaway from this chapter: develop maturity and tact in dealing with contemporaries (or adversaries) and don't let your humility fade when success comes calling. In the face of the rivalry with the Tata Group and the subsequent sectoral overtake, Mr Mahindra downplayed his success. He had the humility, yes, but more importantly, he had the strength of character to accept the statement made by Mr Ratan Tata and recognize him as 'an elder brother'. Exhibiting such grace at a time when he could have easily gloated and declaimed his triumphs to the entire world helped Mr Mahindra warm many hearts. It also gathered an immeasurable amount of goodwill for himself and his business empire.

3
FOCUS ON FRUGAL INNOVATION

USE LOW-COST MODELS FOR INNOVATION AND RESEARCH, ENDEAVOURING TO PROVIDE TAILORED YET COST-EFFECTIVE SOLUTIONS FOR YOUR MARKET

If you were to identify one cornerstone of the M&M Group, which has been behind its sustained success, it would be the approach of using low-cost models for innovation and research. Mr Anand Mahindra has consistently relied on using affordable models that can deliver solutions at a fraction of the cost of foreign technologies. His solutions have not only been inexpensive, but they have also been successful in building relevant solutions for the Indian market.

THE UNDEFEATABLE SCORPIO: A LOW-COST PRODUCTION MARVEL

In the 1990s, Mr Anand Mahindra conducted a meeting with Ford, partners of the M&M Group, to discuss the production of a new sports utility vehicle (SUV), tentatively called Scorpio. The M&M designers showed the prototypes to Mr Alex Trotman, the CEO of Ford at the time. However, Ford's response wasn't what M&M was expecting; the JV partners recommended that M&M do all the work themselves as that would turn out to be cheaper! What Ford recommended did hold weight; after all, it was unlikely that an American company would be able to offer them lower costs than those they could achieve indigenously. Around this time, Mr Mahindra was also trying to convince Ford to set up a JV for R&D—a deal from which Ford could reap remarkable benefits. But the chairman again suggested that M&M go solo and that their JV focus only on manufacturing.[17]

Mr Anand Mahindra took the recommendation in his stride. M&M went ahead with the project, which eventually turned out to be the rugged, low-cost and immensely popular SUV Scorpio. It was launched in 2002. Within a few years of its launch, the project increased the market capitalization of the company by over fifty times.[18]

---

[17] Thomas Stewart and Anand Raman, 'Finding a Higher Gear', *Harvard Business Review*, July-August 2008, accessed November 2018. https://hbr.org/2008/07/finding-a-higher-gear

[18] Neil Munshi, 'Mahindra: flying high?' *Financial Times*, September 15, 2011, accessed October 17, 2018, https://www.ft.com/content/149fc275-537a-3155-ae05-f53c4f6f3a2f

Mr Mahindra admitted it himself—the chairman of Ford had displayed incredible foresight. Scorpio had been designed within a cost of $150 million, only a fraction of the cost it would have taken the foreign manufacturers to develop it. A famous CEO, in an unconfirmed anecdote, is said to have remarked once: 'The M&M cost of $120 million development for the Scorpio was 20 per cent of the cost it would have taken us to make!' And indeed, the new automotive platform had been launched at what was perhaps the lowest cost in the world.

ENCOURAGING INNOVATION THROUGH MAVERICKS AND SKUNKWORKS

The incident with Ford and Scorpio had taught a vital lesson to Mr Anand Mahindra—the importance of lowering costs. He recognized that to compete with the world's best companies, M&M needed to churn out many pathbreaking products like Scorpio at the lowest cost to the company. In short, Mr Mahindra realized that M&M required to be innovative.[19] He devised an effective way to usher in a culture of innovation in the group: encouraging mavericks and skunkworks.

---

[19] Thomas Stewart and Anand Raman, 'Finding a Higher Gear', *Harvard Business Review*, July-August 2008, accessed November 2018. https://hbr.org/2008/07/finding-a-higher-gear

> ### Who are mavericks?
>
> They are people who think and work differently.
>
> ### What are skunkworks?
>
> They are small projects that exist in large organizations, often unapproved by the top management but carried on 'under the radar' by a handful of committed employees. This focus group of employees, usually excellent at networking, devotes its energies to such projects using resources borrowed from other departments in the company.

As a leader connected to his team, Mr Mahindra decided to tap into the power of mavericks and skunkworks. In 1992, he made a conscious decision to start encouraging such projects as a quick yet reliable solution to usher in innovation.

But aren't such projects and covert employee-groups dangerous to the company's culture? No—as long as the company and its leader understand how to channel them for success. Many companies encourage skunkworks because they allow the employees to work on projects after their own hearts—projects that may not have received open support, especially if they threatened to cannibalize or compete with the company's prime offering(s). The kind of freedom and passion that come with a skunkwork do wonders for employee performance and creativity. Moreover, many of these projects can be integrated into the mainstream if they turn out to be successful.

In an article in the July-August 2008 issue of the *Harvard Business Review*, Mr Anand Mahindra cited two examples of disruptive experiments that he encouraged, both of which turned out to be very successful in developing innovative ideas for the business.[20]

1. Fixing frequent breakdowns in utility vehicles

It was the year 1992. Mr Sandesh Dahanukar, a relatively unknown R&D engineer, was facing a problem at work every day. The M&M utility vehicles he worked with would frequently break down. The breakdown would lead to additional costs for the division as well as run down the reliability of the product. There was one straightforward solution to fix this problem: buy new presses and manufacture a stronger chassis. But it was an expensive solution; the new presses would require M&M to invest an additional ₹300 million ($7.50 million) in the division. Was there something else they could do?

Mr Dahanukar proposed an alternative solution to Mr Mahindra—a solution that wasn't run-of-the-mill but could produce exactly the results they needed. What if M&M tried to develop a tubular chassis themselves? Mr Dahanukar had seen a similar chassis during his interactions with global automobile companies. If M&M managed to make this happen, the group would not have to purchase the presses. It would save a tremendous amount of money. Traditionally,

---

[20] Thomas Stewart and Anand Raman, 'Finding a Higher Gear', *Harvard Business Review*, July-August 2008, accessed November 2018. https://hbr.org/2008/07/finding-a-higher-gear

cars were made using a ladder-type chassis, which was like a two-dimensional structure (roughly shaped like a ladder) around which the car was built. It was typically used in heavy commercial vehicles like trucks and buses. A tubular chassis is a three-dimensional hollow tube structure, which is supposedly more rugged and safer, and is used in racing cars and all-terrain vehicles.[21]

Mr Anand Mahindra encouraged Mr Dahanukar to work on a prototype. He authorized an initial budget of ₹600,000 ($15,000) along with complete autonomy. Mr Mahindra realized that Mr Dahanukar was a maverick who worked best alone. He committed to incrementally increasing the investment depending on the progress of the project.

Initially, the progress was slow. But by 1994, Mr Dahanukar had managed to develop a successful prototype along with a whole new manufacturing process. The manufacturing process is still in use in M&M today. Rough calculations indicate that the in-house innovation saved the organization almost ₹299 million ($7.47 million)!

2. Developing a multipurpose vehicle for farmers

In the 1990s, Mr K.J. Davasia, the Head of M&M's tractor sector at the time, came up with an interesting idea. What if M&M developed a multipurpose vehicle that farmers could use for purposes besides working on their farms?

---

[21]'What is a chassis and what are its types?' Accessed March 12, 2019. https://carbiketech.com/chassis/

The idea instantly clicked with Mr Anand Mahindra. He instructed Mr R.N. Nayak, the Head of R&D in the tractor division, to develop a prototype for such a vehicle. He sanctioned an initial budget of ₹1 million ($25,000). Mr Nayak, also a maverick like Mr Dahanukar, worked alone in a vendor's workshop for almost a year. When he finally delivered, he had managed to produce a concept prototype, drawings and adequate components to create a prototype vehicle. Such was his dedication towards the project that he had acquired the components from his colleagues.

Although Mr Mahindra was pleased to see the outcome of Mr Nayak's efforts, the project somehow got relegated to the backburner. For a while, it seemed as if the project would never get the attention it deserved, like some skunkworks are fated to be. But when the vehicle was finally mass-produced in 2006 under the brand name 'Shaan', it became a huge hit. In June 2007, the American Society of Agricultural and Biological Engineers awarded Shaan the prize for the year's most innovative engineering product for the food and agriculture industries.

Mr Anand Mahindra is convinced of the crucial role that mavericks play in the process of innovation. He has religiously found novel ways to harness their talent and enthusiasm along with supporting their efforts to strengthen M&M's formal product-development procedures.

C-NM5: THE LOW-COST AIRCRAFT

The methodology of seeking low-cost innovations transcends sectors in M&M. In 2011, Mr Anand Mahindra exhibited this approach in the aircraft sector, with the introduction of C-NM5, a small, five-seater aircraft introduced by Mahindra Aerospace in a public-private partnership with the National Aerospace Laboratories in India. This aircraft, along with four prototypes, were built at a cost of less than $15 million. Designed with the help of Gipps Aero, the Australian subsidiary of Mahindra Aerospace, this small aircraft was a testimony to the applicability of the low-cost innovation model in a wide gamut of industries. This groundbreaking innovation in an otherwise untapped market gave the company plenty of reasons to be optimistic about the relevance of its strategy in the changing world.

> **The Innovation Rulebook**
>
> In an article for the *Harvard Business Review*, Mr Anand Mahindra listed the essential factors he considered instrumental in encouraging innovation at M&M.[22] The factors are simple yet potent weapons in the hand of any visionary business leader.
>
> 1. Get insights from the customer. New products or

---

[22]Thomas Stewart and Anand Raman, 'Finding a Higher Gear', *Harvard Business Review*, July-August 2008, accessed November 2018. https://hbr.org/2008/07/finding-a-higher-gear

> processes cannot be launched unless one can identify the need for them.
> 2. Great design is essential for great products.
> 3. Encourage experimentation.
> 4. Hire people who do not listen to you. (Interestingly enough, Mr Mahindra claims he always seems to recruit such people!)
> 5. Encourage failures often. Encourage failures early. Put in place a sandbox where people can experiment.
> 6. Ensure that innovations add value to the bottom line.
> 7. Prepare a convincing sales plan to package and market the innovation.

TRANSFORMING SATYAM THROUGH FRUGAL INNOVATION

It wasn't only to in-house projects that Mr Anand Mahindra applied his approach of frugal innovation; he also ensured it covered any acquisitions or takeovers made by M&M. When M&M took over Satyam, an Indian IT services company based in Hyderabad, the host of organizational challenges in the company became evident. Mr Mahindra noted that fiscal discipline was absent in Satyam. Many project incomes were inflated to show higher margins. He quickly calculated that M&M needed to control costs and optimize performance, to finally boost quality.

Soon after the takeover, a culture of reason and prudence replaced the erstwhile one of unnecessary affluence in Satyam. Mr Mahindra ensured that vehicles like Scorpio, Xylo and Verito were sent to receive clients, instead of hiring a Mercedes-Benz or a BMW as had been the practice earlier. Team parties and events at boutique hotels were replaced by parties hosted on campus. Many long-term leases signed by the former promoters in India and abroad were terminated early if they were not deemed profitable. The employees were trained and re-conditioned to think like business people whose ultimate aim was to enhance productivity.

These small but significant steps showed instant results. Soon, the day-to-day operations at Satyam were being completed at one-tenth of the previous cost! Over a two-year period, the principle of frugality initiated by M&M saved Satyam ₹600 crore. The profit margins rose to 21 per cent in September 2012—a massive jump from the earlier 15 per cent.[23]

INNOVATIONS REQUIRE A LEVEL OF DISRUPTION

To continue to be relevant in the rapidly changing business environment, it isn't enough to be innovative; it is equally important to cut costs while working on innovations. To realize this tricky but profitable solution of low-cost innovations, Mr Anand Mahindra has led many experiments within M&M. He is not averse to taking on challenges and coming up with locally relevant solutions, even if this means sanctioning and

---

[23] Kunal N. Talgeri, 'Inside the Merger!' *Fortune India*, December 5, 2012, last accessed February 18, 2019. https://www.fortuneindia.com/technology/inside-the-merger/100760

steering experiments that other business people might label disruptive and dangerous.

Professor Vijay Govindarajan, a professor at the Tuck School of Business, Dartmouth, once stated that teams like these, working on such experiments, are needed to solve India's most urgent problems like housing, health, education, energy and transport.[24] He also applauded the foresight and strength that the M&M Group had shown to become global and innovative, and rise from an $8 billion company to an $80 billion company. Indian companies that had excelled in providing low-cost solutions to customers (whether Western or Indian) at the top of the pyramid, now needed to solve the problems faced by the people at the middle and bottom of the pyramid. In Professor Govindarajan's words, Indian companies had a unique opportunity to solve the problems of every Indian by frugal innovations, and thus become global leaders.[25] M&M's ability to think and act frugally has helped it to achieve precisely this. The low costs have also helped the group to grow more competitive, beat competitors in price wars, and hence ensure long-term survival.

It is significant to note that Mr Anand Mahindra appreciates the need to encourage creative geniuses to keep the wheel of frugal innovation well oiled and running without hiccups. For M&M to be innovative and win against global

---

[24] Vijay Govindarajan, 'Innovation is the key', *Business Today*, October 21, 2011. Accessed on November 8, 2018. https://www.businesstoday.in/opinion/columns/innovation-vijay-govindarajan/story/18640.html
[25] Ibid.

auto giants, the group needed to create a culture where original thinkers are sheltered, encouraged and nurtured. If required, they are given the liberty to work alone so that their creative vision can flourish. This unique trade-off between individual contribution and team effort is a notable aspect of Mr Mahindra's leadership style.

An irksome challenge that gets many companies down on the route to innovation is the burden of compliance. Frequently, companies claim to encourage creativity, but they also require all their employees to conform to standard operating procedures and policies. While organizational discipline is imperative, it is critical to make adjustments if it stifles innovation.

As a leader, Mr Mahindra understands that he needs to allow exceptions for innovation to flourish. He has demonstrated wisdom and intuition in allowing mavericks to operate independently on projects directly approved by him. This approach serves two purposes: one, it keeps the project costs low, since he releases additional funds based on the progress of the project; and two, it reduces risk, since the company does not need to invest too much by way of workforce or time in these projects (that may well be dropped if they do not succeed). Fortunately for Mr Mahindra, his experiments have usually borne fruit, and no drastic measures have been warranted. But if experiments were to fail, he has established a well-padded system that can absorb the outcome and spring back with full gusto.

As more and more companies understand the need for

innovation, newer models and approaches are coming up on the Indian business scene. However, many companies continue to be short-sighted. In their endeavour to optimize production and reduce costs, they put in tremendous corporate effort in eliminating waste and focusing on return on investments. This has an unwelcome consequence: many projects that are hailed 'uncertain' or 'risky' do not get funded. This defeats the very purpose of innovation; all it does is keep the said companies in the illusory bubble that they, at least, *tried* to innovate.

The departmental hierarchy in many business houses also proves to be counter-intuitive for frugal innovation. It is popularly believed that R&D is best left to the R&D department; other departments are disinclined to spare any resources to fuel efforts at innovation. Expending time and money towards free thinking, they feel, would impact their profitability. Therefore, most modern-day organizations continue to be hostile towards skunkworks. These projects have to depend on the motivation of the mavericks, who, although they prefer to work alone, might feel suffocated in being forced to 'collaborate' with their colleagues.

Some companies, however, have woken up to the reality of this convoluted situation and started implementing a friendly platform for original ideas. Google, the American multinational technology company, allows its engineers to work on personal projects for about 20 per cent of their daily time at work. This 'liberty' has resulted in numerous popular products for

Google including Google News, Gmail and AdSense.[26]

In initiating a congenial atmosphere for innovative albeit off-the-beaten-road projects in his company, Mr Anand Mahindra has displayed brilliant foresight. His actions indicate that he understands the reality of competition only too well. As competition heats up, the *only* way companies can stay afloat, let alone thrive, is by being able to attract, retain and encourage innovators. Under Mr Mahindra's leadership, M&M has defined the best way forward for many business establishments of our times.

---

[26]Jillian D'onfro, 'The truth about Google's famous '20% time' policy', *Business Insider*, April 17, 2015, accessed March 2, 2019 https://www.businessinsider.in/The-truth-about-Googles-famous-20-timepolicy/articleshow/46962732.cms

4

ONLY THE PARANOID SURVIVE

IN BUSINESS, A FAIR DOSE OF PARANOIA IS HEALTHY;
SEEK TO BETTER YOUR BUSINESS THROUGH INNOVATION,
DISRUPTION OR ACQUISITION

Only the Paranoid Survive, the title of a book by an American businessman called Andrew Grove, adequately describes the mindset that Mr Anand Mahindra has developed within the M&M Group. That's not to say the M&M premises are dark, forbidding and constantly pushing you to look behind your back. Nonetheless, there *is* a constant push in M&M—the tendency to push the envelope. Mr Mahindra may not be paranoid, but he has embedded systems and processes within his group that (almost) guarantee protection from the invading forces of competition and environmental challenges. These processes are threefold and, sometimes, even involve the risk of becoming one's competitor.

1. Innovate
2. Disrupt
3. Acquire

Mr Mahindra seeks to expand his business by one of the above strategies: innovating across sectors and products, disrupting the market with new products and technologies, and acquiring other companies for rapid growth.

MANTRAS TO DEFEAT PARANOIA: BLUE CHIP CONFERENCES

In 2002, Mr Anand Mahindra organized an annual conference where he addressed his top managers and listened to their ideas for the growth of this business. This was called the **Blue Chip Conference (BCC)**. Annually since then, he has conducted this conference without fail, using the platform to announce the mantra for the year. The said mantra aims at organizing the group around a desired objective and offering rock-solid solutions for beating the looming ghost of business paranoia.

For the 2001 BCC, Mr Mahindra sought to identify characteristics that were common to leading global companies. His research revealed the following unifying traits:[27]

- The aspiration to be global leaders

---

[27] Thomas Stewart and Anand Raman, 'Finding a Higher Gear', *Harvard Business Review*, July-August 2008, accessed November 2018. https://hbr.org/2008/07/finding-a-higher-gear

- The potential to be global leaders
- An emphasis on innovation
- A relentless focus on financial returns

He formulated these characteristics into personalized mantras as follows:[28]

- Strive to become number 1 or number 2 in your industry.
- One-fifth of the revenues must come from products or services introduced in the past four years. There must be globalization metrics for each sector.
- Introduce metrics for return on capital employed (ROCE).
- Introduce metrics for free cash flow (FCF).

At the conference in 2001, all the senior managers had to commit to pursuing these mantras; indeed, if they were unable to meet the required financial targets, their businesses would be folded up. For Mr Anand Mahindra, innovation was a force that needed to be unleashed across the board—in products, processes and services. It was a constructive form of paranoia that fuelled this endeavour; it was the desire to pre-empt, to be proactive at rising to the top instead of waiting to battle with competing forces to accomplish this mission.

At the sixth BCC held in Kuala Lumpur in December

---

[28]Thomas Stewart and Anand Raman, 'Finding a Higher Gear', *Harvard Business Review*, July-August 2008, accessed November 2018. https://hbr.org/2008/07/finding-a-higher-gear

2007, Mr Mahindra administered a classroom exercise with Mr Stefan Thomke, a professor at Harvard Business School, and an expert on technology and product innovation. He conducted a case study on customer-centric innovation—the mantra for the year. It was during this conference that Mr Mahindra set in place the five mantras that would long hold the M&M Group in good stead. The mantras were:

1. Leadership
2. Globalization
3. A ruthless focus on financial services
4. Leadership in every business segment
5. Customer centricity

Speaking at the conference, Mr Mahindra said:[29]

> We've had five fat years, but I foresee uncertainty and discontinuity looming on the horizon. There's the rise of China, the strengthening rupee and surging oil prices. How do we become a zero trauma company? To survive, we've got to bring innovation back on top of our agenda. There are five mantras, namely leadership, globalization, a ruthless focus on financial services, leadership in every business segment and customer centricity. These are our beacons.

---

[29] John Pearce, Richard Robinson and Amita Mital, 'Strategic Management: Formulation, Implementation and Control', page 371.

STRATEGIES ANNOUNCED IN BLUE CHIP CONFERENCES (2002–03)

2002

- **Business leadership:** Be number 1 or 2 in your industry.
- **Innovation:** One-fifth of revenues must come from products or services introduced in the past four years.
- **Globalisation:** Have bespoke metrics for each sector.
- **Financial returns:** Have bespoke metrics for ROCE and FCF.

2003

- **Good to Great:** Move from good to great by insulating the company from volatility (zero trauma) and achieving full potential (stretch goals).

Source: Mahindra upbeat about business in Africa" Autoguide, December 12, 2013. Accessed November 13, 2018. http://www.autoguideindia.com/detail-Mahindra_Group_upbeat_about_business_in_Africa.htm
Pavan Lall, "Anand Mahindra, adventure capitalist", *Fortune India*, December 5, 2010. Accessed November 11, 2018. https://www.fortuneindia.com/people/anand-mahindra-adventure-capitalist/101132

Periodically, M&M conducted in-depth assessments to observe the changes effected by the mantra-based strategy. The results were evident and extremely promising. Particularly encouraging were the following observations that go a long way in proving just how healthy Mr Anand Mahindra's 'paranoia' had turned out to be!

1. Every company within the group set out to be the best in their segments and rank among the top three of their respective sectors. Companies had to innovate and reinvent themselves at every point by anticipating change.
2. The customer became the central protagonist and customer centricity the yardstick by which change and performance were measured.
3. Moreover, employees, right down to the juniormost members, were inspired to outperform in their sphere of influence.
4. Quality and cost leadership transformed into not mere goals, but kaizens to be followed, from corporate cabinets to shop floors across Mahindra facilities globally.

Today, the Blue Chip mantras are an integral part of the DNA of every member of the M&M Group. They form an important aspect of all the business undertaken by the group.[30]

---

[30] John Pearce, Richard Robinson, Amita Mital "Strategic Management: Formulation, Implementation and Control" 2017, McGraw Hill Education, 12th Edition, page 371.

ESTABLISHING SHADOW BOARDS

The concept of shadow boards isn't novel; it is an internationally adopted idea practised by many global corporations like Unilever and General Electric (GE). In 2003, Mr Anand Mahindra also took the shadow board approach to help his business prosper in the light of increasing economic and environmental turbulence.

So, what is a shadow board? It is a group of seven promising young managers, all below thirty-five years, who are handpicked in each company or division of M&M. This group is then asked to consider itself as another management committee, with similar roles and expectations. For two years, this committee deliberates on certain topics of relevance to the business and finally makes recommendations. The issues are amazingly diverse: from new lines of business for the group, to strategic partnerships and matters of governance. The recommendations are made at the annual BCC and presented to the senior management. It is then up to the top management to accept, reject or retain these recommendations for future use. But one thing is for certain: all the proposals are carefully considered by the senior management.

Mr Anand Mahindra initiated shadow boards in M&M with one objective in mind: to 'hear the voice of the young.'[31]

---

[31] Lijee Philip and Kala Vijayraghavan, 'Mahindra group follows management practice of shadow boards,' *The Economic Times*, July 15, 2010, accessed March 12, 2019. https://economictimes.indiatimes.com/news/company/corporate-trends/mahindra-group-follows-management-practice-of-shadow-boards/articleshow/6169552.cms

He staunchly believed that the young personnel in his company had creative, original ideas that could not only curb competition but also fuel faster and meaningful growth. He did not want these original ideas to be drowned out by the bureaucracy or be ignored by the senior managers. To implement the shadow boards in M&M, he restructured the organization to include one more circle in the management tier. This simple initiative ensured that the voice of the young, rising talent was heard in the top decision-making echelons. The marvels it did for the morale of those chosen is a story in and of itself.

Over the years, the shadow boards have come up with many valuable recommendations that have helped M&M achieve the position it currently holds. Many of the recommendations made by these boards have been adopted by the management. Thanks to their inputs, the company has implemented a round-the-clock helpline and a personal approach to distributing increments—steps that have strengthened the human resources of the business. It was also the suggestion of the shadow board that M&M move into commercial vehicles since many of their multi-utility vehicle buyers were also purchasing commercial vehicles. The shadow board believed that the goodwill of the Mahindra brand could be leveraged to sell to these buyers. This recommendation was successfully executed with the Navistar trucks—the group's foray into the commercial vehicles segment.

Mr Anand Mahindra decided to experiment with shadow boards at a time when few other companies in the Indian subcontinent were willing to explore something as drastic as a pseudo-managerial layer. Even though Unilever and GE did use this concept for a time, they abandoned the strategy quickly, choosing to explore other—arguably more traditional—solutions for innovation. But M&M has been able to use the methodology effectively for over eight years, ever since the first board was formed in 2003 (with a two-year tenure).

Today, these boards are reconstituted every year, with 50 per cent new members. The objective remains the same: to bring in fresh ideas, sharpen the good ones and weed out what is outdated. Mr Anand Mahindra personally ensures that the shadow board has access to resources from across the company. Occasionally, a few senior managers are also roped in to mentor the members of these shadow boards and optimize their potential.

CHOOSE PARANOIA OVER COMPLACENCY

In the business world, it isn't success that is the most elusive. Many global organizations manage to achieve success after some degree of struggle in defeating competition and attracting customers' attention. But it is *retaining* this success that is challenging; it is a gift that gets bestowed upon only those who are wise enough to choose paranoia over complacency.

When success visits, many organizations choose to rest on their laurels. The success breeds lethargy and arrogance—behaviours that lead them to ignore newer competitors. Jim Collins, an American business consultant and author, who believes that good is the enemy of great, said that it '...is one of the key reasons why we have so little that becomes great. We don't have great schools, principally because we have good schools. We don't have great government, principally because we have good government. Few people attain great lives, in large part because it is just so easy to settle for a good life.'[32]

His statement holds tremendous meaning for business entities; it implies that complacency in 'good' organizations prevents them from achieving greatness. This is true not only for organizations but is also applicable to people; successful people often suffer the same fate when past success stops them from visualizing the steep, forbidding mountains hidden in the mists.

Mr Anand Mahindra has taken great care to keep the disease of complacency away from his business. He has continuously maintained a constant watch on the changes in the business environment in which M&M operates. Subjecting the entire organization to periodic reviews by internal teams helps him assess potential threats and evaluate future possibilities well in time. This continuous monitoring equips his managers to safeguard their businesses. It also helps the managers evaluate their capabilities and skill set from time to time, and also if these would still be relevant in the future. If they perceive a misfit or lag, Mr Mahindra helps provide necessary training programmes and guidelines to let them

---

[32]Jim Collins, 'Good to Great: Why Some Companies Make the Leap... and Others Don't', *Harper Business*, 2001, page 1.

upgrade their skills and pick up new capabilities.

Another significant takeaway from this chapter is the nifty and customized manner in which Mr Anand Mahindra has adopted the institution of shadow boards. The strategy has enabled M&M to reach out to young talent within the organization and create a sandbox for experimenting with original ideas. Much of this talent might have otherwise been lost due to the absence of a communication channel with the top management. The concept has enabled M&M to retain exceptional talent within the organization and reduce the likelihood of losing such employees to attrition fuelled by stifling bureaucracy and frustration.

In the process, the employees in the shadow board also receive indirect training to become managers of the next generation. Not only does presenting their recommendations infuse them with confidence and a wider understanding of the functioning of the business, but it also increases their exposure to the workings of the top management. In turn, senior management has a glorious opportunity to identify future leaders for various roles. Since Mr Anand Mahindra takes a personal interest in this initiative, it helps drive the right message across the organization, ensuring the complete attention and support of the senior leadership.

5
BE RUTHLESSLY COMPETITIVE

IN THE FACE OF COMPETITION AND A CHANGING
ENVIRONMENT, DON'T HESITATE TO TAKE TOUGH CALLS
TO CEMENT THE FUTURE OF YOUR BUSINESS

In his pursuit of greater competitiveness for M&M, Mr Anand Mahindra provides his group with clear objectives to be achieved. Sometimes, these objectives seem lofty; at other times, they seem outright ruthless. But in the long run, the ruthless approach towards competition has proved to be beneficial for M&M.

PREPARING M&M TO FACE LIBERALIZATION AND GLOBALIZATION

Mr Anand Mahindra's battles with low performance and the need to be steadfast in countering them began early in his career. As we discussed in Chapter 1, he was appalled to see the state of low productivity in M&M in 1992–93, compared to the far superior results achieved by companies like Maruti. One of the first tough decisions he took to attain competitive gains was linking Diwali bonuses to productivity. It was an unpopular decision that earned him the wrath of most of the labour force and threatened to affect his safety and security in the M&M Group. However, as we have seen, the hard-hitting decision ultimately bore results, with the productivity gains rising by almost 150 per cent over a three-year period.

Ever since that first move back in the 1990s, Mr Mahindra has worked tirelessly on aligning his company's operations with the objectives he has outlined for his business. His undaunted desire to rise above the competition is especially apparent in the way he built M&M to face the challenges of the liberalization and globalization of the Indian economy. It was a serious threat indeed, for companies like M&M, which had earlier operated in monopolistic environments with closed economies, were now raw and exposed to the machinations of smarter, sharper and possibly better-endowed global players. The opening up of the economy wasn't the only challenge to overcome either; the economic reforms had allowed a freer import of technologies, which meant even local players had the capabilities to outbid well-entrenched businesses.

To face the threats of liberalization, Mr Mahindra rolled out some massive changes within his business.

- He restructured the group into six sectors, as discussed in the introductory chapter. The restructuring brought in a sense of organization within the company, letting each sector (and sectoral managers) concertedly focus on boosting profitability.
- He moved out of some industries where he saw limited future scope. Some of the sectors Mr Anand Mahindra exited from include oil drilling and instrumentation.
- M&M also brought in new people with fresh ideas to invigorate the business with purposeful tact and brilliant strategies. The environment was more competitive than M&M had experienced in its history so far, and dealing with the new dynamics would require original thought. Mr Anand Mahindra also rationalized the headcount within the organization to a number that was leaner and better suited to work in the swiftly transforming landscape.[33]
- He re-engineered business processes and invested in IT to give M&M a clear technological edge.

In brainstorming these changes, Mr Anand Mahindra was guided by his research on successful companies around the world, as shared by him in 2001 in the *Harvard Business Review*[34]. The primary consideration for M&M at the time

---

[33] Thomas Stewart and Anand Raman, 'Finding a Higher Gear', Harvard Business Review, July-August 2008, accessed November 2018. https://hbr.org/2008/07/finding-a-higher-gear

[34] Ibid.

was to be innovative, develop and act upon the aspiration to be leaders in their businesses, showcase global potential, and adamantly focus on financial returns. In a conference held for his senior executives in 2002 (the first BCC), Mr Mahindra announced these guidelines in the form of rules or mantras that everyone had to follow. He added a rather threatening disclaimer to the announcement: unless these mantras were followed to a T and the financial targets met, the company would be closed down.

As we discussed in Chapter 4, Mr Anand Mahindra steered the efforts of the organization towards set goals in subsequent BCC from 2003 to 2013 and beyond—from innovation and customer centricity to increasing revenues and profits. The concerted focus worked, as did the threat, for M&M started experiencing a turnaround within a year of the first BCC in 2002. Almost every company in the group recorded increased profits and cash flows.

RELY ON WELL-DEVELOPED GOALS AND A SOLID TEAM

In seeking to make his company operationally efficient, Mr Anand Mahindra has occasionally been perceived as being tough-headed. But his ruthlessness has rubbed off well on the fortunes of the group, proving that some decisions, tough as they may be, *have* to be taken.

It is Mr Mahindra's conviction that competition must be dealt with seriously, armed with the support of a team of capable professionals and the reliability of well-developed, focused goals. With these two things in the kitty, a business leader must not hesitate from taking tough calls to secure the future of his or her business, especially in a volatile environment.

6
EMPOWER YOUR TEAM WITH FREEDOM & SUPPORT

ONCE YOU BUILD A CAPABLE TEAM, ALLOW IT TO OPERATE INDEPENDENTLY. BUT ENSURE TO STAND BY IT, SHOULD IT EVER FAIL

At the helm of M&M is a crack team of capable professionals, carefully developed over time by Mr Anand Mahindra. In his role as a business leader, he encourages this team to operate independently and take major decisions, even when some of these decisions involve substantial risks. While his conviction in his team allows him the confidence to grant it independence, he is also proactive in lending them support and positivity, should the team fail for any reason.

STAYING LOYAL TO THE AUTOMOTIVE SECTOR

Mr Pawan Goenka, the Group's MD, who started as the General Manager (GM) R&D in 1993, had joined with a sense of purpose: a master plan he wanted to execute for the organization. Mr Goenka shared his plan with Mr Anand Mahindra, explaining that there were two options he recommended for the growth of the business: one, tweak an existing project; or two, create a new product. Mr Mahindra found the second option optimal, even though it would entail an investment of approximately ₹600 crore. At the time, the revenue of the group was approximately ₹4,000 crore with total profits of ₹250 crore. In this scenario, such a massive investment would mean a tremendous risk. Was it worthwhile or would it eat into the company's fortunes? Mr Mahindra, however, had reasons to believe in his decisions. While explaining his strategy to the Board, he said: 'We have two routes before us. One is that we do not pursue the project and die a natural death. The other is that we go ahead with the project and, if we fail, we die a sudden death. I prefer taking the second route.'[35]

The second route is what M&M ended up taking, and the only thing that died was scepticism. In 1993, M&M tied up with Ford for the manufacture of Escort in India.[36] The decision

---

[35] V. Keshavdev, 'The Boss Anand Mahindra', *Outlook Business*, July 10, 2015, accessed November 2018. https://www.outlookbusiness.com/specials/the-boss/anand-mahindra-1258
[36] Ibid.

to invest energies and resources in the automotive sector might have resonated with Mr Goenka and Mr Mahindra, but it had been a difficult one to take. As we saw in Chapter 1, the M&M Group had been warned against concentrating on the automotive sector by McKinsey & Company the management consultants that advised Mr Anand Mahindra. Their report had recommended that M&M focus instead on the tractor business, as it would fail to compete against the global competition in the auto sector. By going against the report and believing in the master plan of his senior executive, Mr Mahindra displayed a quiet confidence that is often the precursor of success.

THE TURBULENT TAKEOVER OF SATYAM

In 2009, Mr Anand Mahindra expressed a desire to take over Satyam Computers. Tech Mahindra was interested in merging with Satyam Computers to entrench its feet in the IT sector. Mr Mahindra made an offer to Mr Ramalinga Raju, who was the incumbent chairman and CEO of Satyam Computers. As it turns out, both gentlemen happened to be on the Board of the Indian School of Business (ISB). However, Mr Raju chose not to respond to the proposal.

It was around this time, in 2009, that Satyam Computers found itself embroiled in a shocking scam. The newspapers were flooded with reports on how Mr Raju had manipulated the company's accounts of almost ₹14,162 crore—a confession that shocked the corporate world. It appeared that the potential deal between Tech Mahindra and Satyam had packed up even before it had a chance to see the light of dawn.

But Mr Anand Mahindra had ideas to the contrary. Amidst this turmoil, he trusted only one person to take the optimal decision regarding the possible buyout: Mr Vineet Nayyar, the executive vice chairman of Tech Mahindra. Mr Mahindra asked him only one question: 'Are you confident of pulling it off?'

To this, Mr Nayyar replied, 'Yes.'

'So, what are you waiting for then?' Mr Mahindra is reported to have replied. 'Go ahead and buy it.'[37]

After displaying complete trust in his team and believing that his senior executives thoroughly understood the business and the environment it operated in, Mr Anand Mahindra showed no qualms about picking up the cudgels to cement the decision. He conducted meetings with the board to convince them of the buyout and to address their concerns on the associated risks. He managed to persuade the board by following three simple steps.

1. Convince the board of a strategic fit.
2. Explain the potential risks.
3. Discuss plans to mitigate these risks.

---

[37] V. Keshavdev, 'The Boss Anand Mahindra', *Outlook Business*, July 10, 2015, accessed November 2018. https://www.outlookbusiness.com/specials/the-boss/anand-mahindra-1258

This three-step plan is a succinct way of garnering trust and assurance within the organization. In the case of Satyam, Mr Mahindra discussed at length his plans to integrate it within M&M and restore the customer trust that had been lost after the news of the scam broke.

In the high-risk buyout of a tainted company—a deal that rested on the conviction of one senior executive—Mr Anand Mahindra displayed unflinching support. He showcased the willingness to assure his employees of his backing and also extended it to the board level, thereby guaranteeing minimum resistance. Over time, this has proved to be a quality his people greatly admire.

CHARTING INTERNATIONAL WATERS

Many business leaders find it relatively manageable to empower their team to take local decisions for domestic markets. However, they find it challenging to adopt the same approach while operating in international markets. Mr Hemant Luthra, the chairman of Mahindra CIE since 2018, remembers the time when he had gone on an acquisition spree in Europe. He had bought three companies, namely Stokes Group, Jeco Holdings AG, and Schöneweiss & Co. GmbH. In taking the decisions for these acquisitions, he was fully empowered to trust in his instincts and assessment.

He recalls:[38]

At the time of all these acquisitions worth hundreds of millions of dollars, not once was I asked questions about valuation. I was empowered to figure that out myself in consultation with the CFO, Bharat Doshi. All I was asked was whether I had made sure that it was people we could trust, were our cultures similar, was the technology right and were we getting appropriate customer access.

Soon after the acquisitions, however, Mr Luthra found himself surrounded by a severe calamity—one that had the potential to undermine all the good work done. The Lehman Brothers crisis had turned up to haunt the market; the downfall of Lehman Brothers was one of the most massive bankruptcies in the history of the world. But Mr Anand Luthra needn't have worried, for both Mr Anand Mahindra and Mr Keshub Mahindra stood solidly by him. He remembers: 'All that Keshub Mahindra asked was whether I had honestly answered the questions before going in for the acquisitions. He said, "We should hang in there—this, too, shall pass, as have many other crises in my experience."'

Supporting his uncle, Mr Anand Mahindra said, 'I am glad that the captain of the ship did not panic and steered it to safety.'[39]

---

[38] V. Keshavdev, 'The Boss Anand Mahindra', *Outlook Business*, July 10, 2015, accessed November 2018. https://www.outlookbusiness.com/specials/the-boss/anand-mahindra-1258
[39] Ibid.

Mr Mahindra's ability to put his people ahead of himself also served him in good stead when the forgings business of the group was in acquisition mode. A few years after the European acquisitions, the group set up Mahindra CIE. It was an establishment with a unique governance structure. Mahindra had sold what later became Mahindra CIE, to CIE Automotive, the Spanish group dealing in auto components, by taking shares of the latter (an equity swap). This way, CIE Automotive became the largest shareholder of Mahindra CIE, and M&M became the second largest shareholder of CIE Automative.[40] The structure shared the benefits from the rise in the valuation of the equity with both the European managers and sellers. The governance structure caught the eye of not only domestic market observers but also dignitaries from around the globe. Mr Anand Mahindra was invited to address a seminar on 'Asia: Threat or Opportunity' hosted by Ms Angela Merkel, the chancellor of Germany at the time. The seminar was to be held at Bundestag, and top corporate luminaries from around the world were invited. Mr Mahindra refused the invitation. Instead, he asked Mr Luthra to go in his place to address the gathering.

Mr Luthra still recalls the exact words of his leader: 'You are the architect; you should go in my place and take credit for what you have done.' Mr Luthra felt that this gesture, showing

---

[40]Shally Seth Mohile, 'Mahindra CIE looking for more acquisitions,' Livemint, September 26, 2016, accessed March 12, 2019. https://www.livemint.com/Industry/gSAbxt096c1Yi98cFxoAOL/Mahindra-CIE-looking-for-more-acquisitions.html

Mr Mahindra's vote of confidence and appreciation, meant more to him than any financial bonuses he could have ever received.

The ease with which Mr Anand Mahindra trusts his people has deep roots: it stems from a cautious assessment of the potential of his employees and the likelihood of success of their proposed strategies. In 2013, when Mr Luthra was heading Systech, the group's component-making division, there was an opportunity to make deep-seated organizational changes. Systech had by then become a ₹4,000 crore venture, with many acquisitions under its belt. Mr Luthra had a brainwave: what if they sold their controlling stake to CIE Automotive? It would yield significant monetary gains and also propel M&M into the big league in the sector.

Mr Anand Mahindra sided with Mr Luthra and proceeded with the deal. The results were impressive, to say the least: M&M received 13.5 per cent of CIE Automotive, earned over ₹2,000 crore, and jumped into the league of the top twenty-five component makers globally. The establishment now makes almost $3 billion in revenues.

Mr V.S. Parthasarathy, the Group CFO since 2013, admits to the incredible strength that emanates from having your leader believe in you. He recalls an incident that happened in 2004, when M&M was planning on entering the South African market through a JV with a local partner. The partner wanted to include the tractor business in the venture. However, M&M had set up the tractor business primarily to engage in the assembly and distribution of vehicles. Mr Parthasarathy was not too keen on going ahead with the JV if this clause had to be honoured. The tractor business in South Africa, he felt, was tiny and not worth the investment. But would the board, especially the chairman, agree with his assessment of the situation?

On the day of the deal, Mr Anand Mahindra once again displayed complete trust in his executive. He backed out of the agreement in its present form. He informed the potential JV partner in simple words that he, Mr Anand Mahindra, was the most powerless person in the room and could not force his team to go along with something that it did not believe in. Eventually, the JV did go through, but exactly as Mr Parthasarathy had desired; only the automotive business of M&M was part of the deal. A few years later, in 2009, M&M took complete control of the venture by increasing their stake from 51 per cent to 91 per cent.

Mr Parthasarathy reports that Mr Mahindra has never failed to value the recommendations of his team members, always trusting the force of his empowerment and the importance of liberty. According to Mr Parthasarathy, the guiding principle that Mr Mahindra follows is very simple: 'He empowers you, asks the right questions, and supports you.'[41]

---

[41] V. Keshavdev, 'The Boss Anand Mahindra', *Outlook Business*, July 10, 2015, accessed November 2018. https://www.outlookbusiness.com/specials/the-boss/anand-mahindra-1258

SAILING THROUGH DOWNTURNS

It would be too optimistic to expect that the people empowered by Mr Anand Mahindra would never make unfruitful decisions or be blessed with a 100 per cent success rate in all their dealings. But it is during downturns that a leader's principles genuinely get tested. Mr Mahindra sets an example worth emulating in this regard, for he has supported his team even when the results have been less than optimal.

Mr Arun Nanda, the non-executive chairman of Mahindra Life Space and Mahindra Holiday, shares an incident that occurred in the first year after the company got listed. After assessing the financial situation, Mr Nanda decided that it would be best to skip paying a dividend. Mr Anand Mahindra did not intervene. He instructed Mr Nanda to take a call, together with the board. Mr Arun Nanda said, '(It) shows not only his style but, more importantly, his trust in people. In fact, the biggest change, personally, for me since Anand came on board is that he has helped me become an entrepreneur and that's how I learnt to take risks.' He added that he has had more autonomy and authority in businesses he ran than many relatives of promoters would have had in family-run businesses.

Mr Nanda was also given full liberty to implement his decisions regarding Mahindra Triton, the hovercrafts business of M&M. After the division had failed to become successful, he recommended to Mr Anand Mahindra and Mr Keshub Mahindra that Triton should be shut down. Both of them encouraged him to think like an entrepreneur and, as long as a decision was well thought out, to go ahead with it without reservation. Mr Anand Mahindra said to him, 'Arun, I am glad you are taking risks. If you succeeded in everything you did, I would have thought you are not taking risks.'[42]

Indeed, the impetus that comes with empowerment and faith has helped drive many new businesses for M&M, such as Club Mahindra, the vacation timeshare business launched in 1996. The group invested over ₹30 crore in the business, which eventually became one with a valuation of over ₹2,000 crore![43] The returns have been splendid, but they may have never materialized had Mr Anand Mahindra failed to trust his team in taking important decisions for a new, previously unexplored line of business.

Mr Rajeev Dubey, the group president of HR and Corporate Services and CEO of the after-market sector, believes that this implicit trust that Mr Anand Mahindra has in his people is the hallmark of his management style. While he follows the basic principle of championing what is good for the business, he doesn't hesitate from willingly giving up control whenever required. Mr Dubey notes, 'He stood by me. He gives credit to people rather than taking it away and that is the sign of a great leader.'

---

[42] V. Keshavdev, 'The Boss Anand Mahindra', *Outlook Business*, July 10, 2015, accessed November 2018. https://www.outlookbusiness.com/specials/the-boss/anand-mahindra-1258
[43] Ibid.

TRUST YOUR EMPLOYEES

In all his business decisions, Mr Anand Mahindra displays one unifying quality: a high degree of trust in and freedom for his people. Mr Anand Mahindra has, evidently, put in painstaking effort to empower his people. Once his teams have been authorized and are running their companies autonomously, he ensures that they have his backing and support. He volunteers to garner approvals from the board for them, whenever the situation demands it.

It is critical to note here that Mr Mahindra goes one vital step ahead of many other managers in the way he channels his people. While many managers are able to attract top talent to their organization, they fail to empower or support them. But this is how the M&M Group is different. Here, those who deserve to be bestowed with power are indeed offered the freedom and the encouragement to perform. As the leader, Mr Anand Mahindra does not constantly peer over the shoulders of his executives. When they achieve success, he does not step forward to receive the credit on their behalf. Instead, he puts them in the limelight and lets them bask in the glory of their performance—a prime motivator for an employee belonging to any rung in the organization.

Mr Anand Mahindra has also retained his entrepreneurial spirit in the manner in which he associates with his people. He encourages his team to take risks because he strongly believes that a company must take calculated risks to make progress. The buzzword here is 'calculated', for measured risks, as opposed to blind risks, have a far greater probability of working out in favour of the business. Such risks present the scope to boost the capabilities and the performance of the company, but if they were to sink, the company would not sink with them. Mr Mahindra promotes the culture of such risk-taking within M&M, persuading his team members to come up with bright ideas and not waving away original thought, like many large establishments are guilty of doing.

It is important here to establish the difference between the two contrasting approaches adopted by different managers: trying new things and being risk-averse. Many managers in leading organizations are completely risk-averse. They do not want to try new things that could 'rock the boat' or compete with what their business is currently doing. Why change something that is proceeding perfectly, to experiment with something that may fall flat on its face? But managers like Mr Mahindra prefer to adopt the first approach—that of giving new ideas a chance, especially when they come from capable executives with a rock-solid understanding of the business. This approach might seem hazardous, but it proves to be safer in the long run. It avoids the dangerous risk of a competitor—someone without any constraints against experimenting—emerging out of the blue and putting the company out of business.

Finally, Mr Anand Mahindra's strategy of siding with his people at all times has another significant lesson: it boosts transparency. In many organizations that are risk-averse and where the leaders penalize managers for failed projects, there is a tendency to fabricate data. Often, managers continue to run such projects despite knowing that they are doomed and have zero chance of success. They keep investing energies into such dwindling projects only because they are afraid to admit to their losses. In such organizations, failures are treated as career suicides—the end of the line for the managers in question. But at M&M, with a risk-friendly culture and the presence of a leader who extends his support even when things are suboptimal, transparency is infinitely higher. When a project looks unlikely to succeed, Mr Anand Mahindra usually leaves the decision to the CEO of the corresponding division. Then, one of two distinct paths is adopted to sustain a culture of honesty and clarity at M&M.

1. If the CEO and his team feel that the dip in performance is temporary, Mr Mahindra expresses a willingness to expand the learning curve and give the project more time to become successful.
2. On the other hand, if the manager feels that the business needs to be folded up, he supports this decision too, not penalizing the manager for taking risks but bolstering his confidence and appreciating his clarity of thought in putting his or her foot down.

This systematic approach has helped Mr Anand Mahindra's team to develop into a group of professionals that understands the essence of risk-taking but has somehow managed to keep its fingers on the pulse of what makes risks tick.

7
NURTURE FUTURE MANAGERS

ORGANIZE TRAINING PROGRAMMES FOR YOUR EMPLOYEES TO INSTIL A KEEN UNDERSTANDING OF THE BUSINESS AND RAISE LEADERS FOR THE FUTURE

We have already discussed how Mr Anand Mahindra has put together a team of qualified professionals at the helm of all his businesses and given them the freedom to operate autonomously in their domains. He offers continued support to their decisions even when they are contrary to the expectations of the board or the opinions of consultants and observers. But from where does his faith in his people emerge? Wouldn't it be foolishly optimistic and generous for a business leader to empower his team with a level of trust so high, without guaranteeing that it is, indeed, worthy?

Mr Anand Mahindra has an effective solution to maintain

his trust in his people: regular training and development programmes.

In an article published in the *Harvard Business Review* 2008, Mr Mahindra famously said[44]: 'They will learn that the company is intellectually open, and it is international in a way that no other enterprise is. I'm not going to pretend that M&M isn't Indian, but it's much more than that. I am building a group where intellect and ideas have no boundaries or nationalities.'

MANAGEMENT DEVELOPMENT PROGRAMME AT HARVARD

In an interview with the *Harvard Business Review*, Mr Anand Mahindra stated that M&M had a strong Indian heritage. Therefore, although he was creating a transnational company, the home country was still India, with its 'capital' in Mumbai. Despite the strong Indian foundation, Mr Mahindra was aware of the needs of the business: attracting and retaining global talent. He had to establish an intellectual 'capital', and he found the perfect spot for it in his alma mater, the globally reputed Harvard University. Mr Anand Mahindra believed that having a university of Harvard's standing as intellectual capital would help him transcend any boundaries of nationality or ethnicity.

Select faculty members from Harvard University visit throughout the year and conduct training programmes for the employees at M&M. Once a year, Mr Anand Mahindra takes

---

[44]Thomas Stewart and Anand Raman, 'Finding a Higher Gear', *Harvard Business Review*, July-August 2008, accessed November 2018. https://hbr.org/2008/07/finding-a-higher-gear

his senior executives on location to Harvard for a week-long executive development programme. The executives of M&M from across the globe attend this programme along with their spouses. At the surface, this training programme helps equip the executives with the necessary skills for conducting their business better, ranging from customer centricity and innovative thought to deriving greater financial returns. However, the programme has an even more meaningful impact: it serves to dispel any apprehensions that his team members may have about the culture at M&M. The Harvard programmes are a sharp statement on the group's international persona and a stark reminder of the fact that M&M is continually striving to be a global company, if it isn't already one.

OTHER TRAINING AND DEVELOPMENT PROGRAMMES

Apart from the sessions conducted by professors and visiting faculty from Harvard University, Mr Anand Mahindra also encourages unique methods for training his executives. His focus lies not only in training his team members in various aspects of the business but also in shaping them to assume leadership positions in the future. Two such standout training programmes that Mr Anand Mahindra has pioneered in his group include:

1. Blue Chip Conferences

These annual conferences are held in various cities around the world. The annual theme is set by Mr Anand Mahindra.

These conferences help align the entire workforce of M&M—who are spread all over the globe—to the essence of M&M's business empire.

Apart from the strategic wins of these conferences, which we discussed in depth in Chapter 4, it is also worth noting their cultural triumphs. At these conferences, the executives of M&M engage in sharing the vision and the objectives of the group, thus bypassing geographical distances and getting motivated to function as a unified whole. This is a fundamental goal for a multinational firm to achieve since it has employees belonging to multiple nationalities and cultures.

2. Shadow Boards

The shadow boards set up by Mr Anand Mahindra, starting in 2003, are also an effective, if subtle, training programme. These boards, originally established to listen to the voice of young managers, slowly train the members to understand the nuances of the business empire. While the board serves as a platform for the chosen employees to test and sharpen their talent, it also doubles as the platform on which the entire senior management at M&M can interact with the managers of the future.

A shadow board is an aspiration within the group; it is a clear solution to avoid being gagged up and getting lost in a complex structure. It is also an opportunity to have yourself heard even when your position in the firm is 'too low'. The young talent at M&M is enthused by the confidence that their work is being valued and their recommendations will be seriously considered. Furthermore, these boards are a validation of an employee's potential and an opportunity to hone it further, even in the scenario of lacking support from line managers.

With time, shadow boards have not only effectively trained bright, young employees at M&M for leadership positions but also helped retain top talent within the organization. Many such employees might have been lost to competitors had M&M failed to install a mechanism to identify and nurture them.

TRUST YOUR EMPLOYEES

A sound manager draws his strength from his team. This becomes possible only if the team is worthwhile enough to fall back on. Mr Anand Mahindra ensures that his team is qualified, capable and constantly learning. His continual efforts at training his team for future challenges is also insulation against competition, attrition and employee dissatisfaction.

Mr Mahindra never fails to organize annual trips to Harvard Business School for his senior management. The sessions conducted at Harvard, which is considered by many to be the best B-school in the world, expose his team to the latest global trends and skill sets. His employees reap the benefit of learning from the world's best teachers and advisors; back home, they have the opportunity to apply their newly acquired knowledge to further business gains. Not many leaders invest such time and effort in exposing their team members to international thought; but then, not many of them receive the bonuses of doing so either. Associating with the finest may be expensive, but here's what M&M gets in return: a world-class army trained in the best global practices to counter challenges of various kinds!

Another benefit of the annual training programmes is the unification they drive among the various layers of leadership spread across the globe. Getting everyone together for a common purpose helps sweep in alignment and goal-clarity. It also increases cohesiveness and camaraderie, which develops a desire to work together towards a common objective.

8
STAY ATTUNED TO YOUR NETWORKS, COMPETENCIES & RISKS

DON'T RELY ON ONE CORE COMPETENCY FOR SUCCESS; INSTEAD, ENDEAVOUR TO BUILD A NETWORK OF STRATEGIC ACTIVITIES

In the business world, many companies have long relied on the popular theory of **core competency**. It has been followed religiously by organizations in various business sectors as a reliable route to success. However, Mr Anand Mahindra has preferred to adopt a different approach—one that goes against this commonly accepted principle.

WHAT IS CORE COMPETENCY?

Core competency is defined as a combination of resources, experiences and skills in an activity that is central to a firm's value-generation approach. A firm may use this said competency to get an advantage in the business landscape. For the chosen competency to work, it is essential that it should be difficult for competitors to either obtain or imitate it.

So, if numerous businesses have successfully leveraged this principle, why has Mr Anand Mahindra opted against it? It is his belief that for lasting success, excelling in one parameter is not adequate. He finds that instead of making one competency the heart and soul of the business, it is preferable to build a network of activities that can provide a strategic advantage. This approach that Mr Mahindra follows for M&M is in line with the **value chain theory** proposed by Michael Porter, a renowned American academician who propounded several theories on economics and business strategy.

WHAT IS VALUE CHAIN THEORY?

This theory states that in any business, the long-term competitive advantage does not necessarily stem from the products it makes. Instead, it arises from the set of distinct activities that a company performs—activities that should be much better than those undertaken by the competitors. It is this set of activities that determines the company's long-term, sustainable competitive advantage. Hence, according to this theory, a company must do two things to achieve success:

1. Seek to ensure that it has a distinct set of activities.
2. Seek to ensure that it continues working on developing and improving these activities continually, in line with the dynamic business environment.

In the changing times, the value chain theory has proved to be more reliable than the core competency theory. This is primarily because even if a business succeeds in building a venerable core competency, it does not insulate them from competitors who also endeavour to improve their offerings and match the best in the market. Therefore, any advantage, no matter how unique, does not last long.

BUILDING FORTRESS MAHINDRA

Mr C.K. Prahalad, the renowned management guru who passed away in 2010, defined Mr Anand Mahindra's business strategy as 'Fortress Mahindra'. In comparing the group with a fortress, Mr Prahalad highlighted the activity system of the business that had become difficult to copy or defeat. Let us take the example of M&M's vehicle business to understand this better.

When Mr Anand Mahindra entered the vehicle business, he viewed the step from a 360-degree perspective. From the outset, he attempted to create relationships that could help the group share purchases, logistics, brands, channels, and efforts at R&D. The idea was to create a fruitful web of relationships that would reap dividends as the business progressed. And indeed, the network helped M&M establish two strong channels in this sector: an automotive channel and an edge in tractors. These two channels gave M&M remarkable brand equity in the rural markets, which, in the early 2000s, were growing by leaps and bounds. Eventually, these channels bolstered the growth of the Scorpio. In 2011, when many competitors faced declining sales, Scorpio managed not only to stay afloat but also do well. This, agrees Mr Anand Mahindra, was only due to rural consumption—a benefit that M&M had cultivated over time.

The strategic advantages of Fortress Mahindra not only emanate from the networks of local suppliers, but also the group's sprawling international presence in over a hundred countries, including the USA and France, and multiple industries of operation.

FEDERATION VS. CONGLOMERATE

In 2008, Mr Anand Mahindra realized a significant structural shift in his business. No matter how profitable M&M became, there was a limit to the number of new businesses it could develop. Why? It followed as a natural consequence and limitation of the group's corporate structure. The structure of M&M at that time limited the potential of new business ideas. Many such ideas could not be evaluated, and the small businesses of the group languished for lack of attention. Mr Anand Mahindra assessed that he must introduce one major change to correct this scenario: he must organize his group as a federation and not a centralized conglomerate.[45]

In emerging markets like India, some business groups have structured themselves as groups of companies or federations. Mr Anand Mahindra feels that such businesses are better equipped to compete than conglomerates that have everything under one company. Organizing M&M in the form of a federation would also help Mr Mahindra follow Michael Porter's network of activities theory (or value chain theory). Finally, it would take the strain off the Mahindra Annual Planning Cycle (MAPC), also called the 'War Room Review'. These review meetings of the entire business were conducted once a month, or sometimes quarterly. The process would eat into the time of the senior management and Mr Mahindra himself. As the business grew, these meetings had become a draining challenge that often proved to be more taxing than rewarding.[46]

Realising that the structural reorganization promised multiple advantages for the future of M&M, Mr Anand Mahindra took a leap of faith. He adapted the restructuring model from private equity (PE) firms operating at the time. During his research, he observed that many leading private equity players managed as many as eighty companies in a

---

[45]Ashish Mishra and Cuckoo Paul, 'Anand Mahindra: The Federator', *Forbes India*, October 28, 2013, last accessed February 18, 2019, http://www.forbesindia.com/article/leaderhip-awards-2013/anand-mahindra-the-federator/36375/1
[46]Ibid.

portfolio. These players utilized **financial engineering** or the application of technical methods from mathematics and computation to manage a business. Mr Mahindra swiftly learnt financial engineering and consolidated the managerial talent in M&M. He also set up Mahindra Partners, a PE firm within the M&M group. This firm would scout for businesses of the future and have an independent point of view, as opposed to the existing, old legacy businesses.

Mahindra Partners has since classified the group companies into three categories:

1. Incubation businesses, like solar businesses and speedboat ventures;
2. Growth capital phase companies that need to find strategic partners or go for an initial public offering (IPO);
3. Pure private equity investments that have been invested in, but with an exit in mind.

The third category of pure private equity investments has not proven easy to run for the group. Many of these businesses (all of which have been funded by M&M) have been riddled with challenges. However, by implementing a classification like this, Mr Anand Mahindra has accomplished an admirable clarity of vision. The eventual purpose is apparent: to strengthen the federation with companies that have promise. To do so, M&M can choose to move the 'good' ones into the federation. It can also choose to monetize some of the companies either by an IPO or a strategic sale.

As of 2019, it has been almost a decade since Mr Anand Mahindra launched the private equity arm and organized his group as a federation. The consequences have been positive. The biggest advantage of the approach has been the padding that all the group companies have received. In a way, each company is now ring-fenced from the damage of failure. Each company is also free to finance its growth and make its mistakes. Ultimately, this supports potentially infinite growth in the federation. M&M remains at the steering wheel as the major shareholder and the spine of the structure, but the former limitation on expansion ceases to exist.

In the reformed structure, it is important to understand Mr Anand Mahindra's role. As the Group Head, he is responsible for both generating and evaluating new ideas that could add value to the federation. Mr Zhooben Bhiwandiwala, the managing partner at Mahindra Partners as of 2019, shares that it is Mr Anand Mahindra who introduces his team to new people and ideas on e-mail. Such introductions come in almost every day. Mr Bhiwandiwala calls him 'the biggest funnel for their ideas.'[47]

At present, Mr Anand Mahindra describes his business to analysts in a charming fashion: 'M&M is a farm

---

[47] Ashish Mishra and Cuckoo Paul, 'Anand Mahindra: The Federator', *Forbes India*, October 28, 2013, last accessed February 18, 2019, http://www.forbesindia.com/article/leaderhip-awards-2013/anand-mahindra-the-federator/36375/1

equipment and automobiles company with a very valuable portfolio of investments.'[48]

MEASURING RISKS FOR CONTINUED SUCCESS

Apart from playing a major role in brainstorming for new ideas, Mr Anand Mahindra also employs a vital weapon to protect his business: **risk measurement**. As the Group Head, he, along with a dedicated team, assesses the risk in all new projects. While Mr Mahindra has a track record of risk-taking, it is worth remembering that all these risks have been *measured*. As opposed to blind risks that belie calculations, his entrepreneurial style relies on measured risk-taking.[49] He considers such calculated risks to be at the root of his new ventures. In fact, he recalls that most of his disappointments in his career so far have stemmed from occasions when he failed to take adequate measured risks. He particularly regrets not taking the risk of investing in a castings plant in 1994. M&M had partnered with the Spanish company Mondragon Corporation, and had even bought land near Pune in Maharashtra, and was all set. But the downturn made them fearful and M&M decided against proceeding with

---

[48]Pavan Lall, 'Anand Mahindra, adventure capitalist', *Fortune India*, December 5, 2010. Accessed November 11, 2018.https://www.fortuneindia.com/people/anand-mahindra-adventure-capitalist/101132
[49]Ashish Mishra and Cuckoo Paul, 'Anand Mahindra: The Federator', *Forbes India*, October 28, 2013, last accessed February 18, 2019, http://www.forbesindia.com/article/leaderhip-awards-2013/anand-mahindra-the-federator/36375/1

the investment. It turned out that the fear was baseless, and M&M missed an opportunity when the market took off. M&M had to endure supply chain constraints over quality castings and this forced it to incur monetary and productivity losses. Mr Mahindra reflects that the castings incident taught him a life lesson he hasn't forgotten since: never to look at investment decisions over a short time frame, but always to keep the long-term outlook in mind.[50]

This is not to say, however, that all risks will be safe to take, even when they fall within estimated measurements. Mr Anand Mahindra has maintained a cautious approach to risk-taking, avoiding going ahead when certain risks become too hot to handle. A case in point is the bidding for Jaguar Land Rover (JLR) in 2007 when M&M was pitted against the Tata Group. While Mr Anand Mahindra was keenly interested in the bid, he opted out of the race when the bidding went higher than his mental benchmark. Sticking adamantly to the racecourse would have been a bigger risk for the group than he was willing to take.

CHOOSE DIFFERENTIATION OVER CORE COMPETENCY

In the present context, businesses must carefully evaluate the guiding principle that will suit their operations best: the

---

[50] Ashish Mishra and Cuckoo Paul, 'Anand Mahindra: The Federator', *Forbes India*, October 28, 2013, last accessed February 18, 2019, http://www.forbesindia.com/article/leaderhip-awards-2013/anand-mahindra-the-federator/36375/1

approach of pursuing a core competency or focusing on a spectrum of activities crucial for the company. Mr Anand Mahindra has chosen the latter and it has turned out to be the optimal path for the M&M Group.

While centring all energies on a core competency does have its merits, the value chain approach is likely to be more relevant in a flexible, competitive atmosphere. If a company chooses to focus on the entire gamut of activities it engages in, instead of prioritizing excellent performance in a single activity or area, it has a better chance of remaining relevant in the market.

Mr Anand Mahindra's business style also teaches entrepreneurs and leaders to adopt a prudent and tempered risk-taking policy. Taking risks to further the business is crucial for growth, but ensuring they are calculated, as opposed to blind, is vital for the survival of the business.

9

CHOOSE YOUR BATTLES CAREFULLY

STAND UP FOR WHAT YOU MUST, PICKING BATTLES
THAT UPHOLD YOUR PRINCIPLES. BUT REMEMBER THAT
CONTROVERSY ISN'T A BUSINESS LEADER'S BEST FRIEND

For a business leader, it isn't adequate to keep tabs on the business landscape; the social and political scenes can have deep-rooted implications on business, and ignoring them can be a leader's biggest mistake. In the turbulent times that we live in, when different people vie for attention on social media and use the digital platform to make their opinions—often biased and prejudiced—heard, what approach should a businessperson adopt? There are multiple battles to be fought in the territories of economic reforms, market conditions and customer reactions to various products, but should a leader opt to wage these battles or maintain distance from the limelight?

Mr Anand Mahindra is distinct from many of his contemporaries in recognizing the need to deal with battles in the social, political and economic landscapes. His strategy is straightforward: do not fight every battle that you encounter, but choose ones that add value to your belief system, stakeholders and business.

Mr Mahindra, for the most part, has remained fairly outspoken in expressing his opinions on Twitter. He has frequently commented on subjects that others in similar positions have dodged for fear of being misquoted or misconstrued.

In 2015, the Reserve Bank of India (RBI) announced something heartening during its monetary review: a significant rate cut. Mr Raghuram Rajan, the RBI governor at the time, had cut the repo rate by twenty-five basis points. This enthused many business owners as well as unfurled euphoria in the market. Mr Mahindra, expressing his happiness publicly on Twitter, wrote, 'Three cheers! The RBI Governor has moved from being "Reluctant Raghu" to "Rate-cut-Raghu!"'

On 4 February 2019,[51] Mr Anand Mahindra posted something acutely personal on his Twitter timeline: his experience of babysitting his one-year-old grandson for a week. Appreciating the efforts of working women in his tweet, he wrote:

> I've been helping to baby-sit my year old grandson this past week & it's brought home to me the stark

---

[51] https://twitter.com/anandmahindra/status/109267548958 6569216

> reality of this image. I salute every working woman & acknowledge that their successes have required a much greater amount of effort than their male counterparts.

In Mr Mahindra's opinion, working women ended up putting in much more effort than their male counterparts. He attached a cartoon with his tweet, depicting a race track with three men and three women at the starting line. The difference among the participants was that the women had laundry, ironing and cooking in their path, but the men had a track free of roadblocks. He warmly saluted every working woman and acknowledged that their successes entailed significantly more effort than the triumphs of their male peers and adversaries. The tweet received a lot of press coverage and appreciation in the media.

While it is evident that Mr Mahindra has been outspoken in commenting on issues that resound with him, it is essential to analyse the tact behind this behaviour. While it is true that he doesn't hold himself back from jumping into conversations or participating in discussions he finds necessary, he also displays great foresight in choosing the said interactions. The topics that he comments on are the outcome of a careful, behind-the-scenes process that derives from his long-term goals for his personal and professional lives. Let us look at two examples.

1. Defending business decisions

In 2018, Mr Anand Mahindra extended his support to Krea University, an educational venture that will focus on liberal arts and science courses. On the sidelines of the launch, the press had some probing questions. Did he, like many other corporate leaders, find himself unwilling to take the government head-on, fearing a negative rub-off on his business? How would the university stay liberal in the backdrop of corporate houses unwilling to challenge the government, fearing an adverse impact on their business interests?

Mr Mahindra was unfazed in his response. He replied to the questions stating that his shareholders did not pay him to make controversial statements. He told the media that he could say what he liked, if he gave up his business and retired. But it was his principle that as long as corporate leaders were paid by their shareholders, they must avoid making statements that could trigger futile controversy.[52]

In justification of the education venture, he commented that corporate houses were equipped to fund and support universities, and this is what M&M was aspiring to do. In fact, he added, corporate houses were better off investing their resources in realms they understood well, instead of squandering time in making controversial statements to get noticed.

In defending his business choices, Mr Anand Mahindra ensured that his defence was well researched and coherent.

---

[52] Masoom Gupta, 'My shareholders pay me to make money, not controversy: Anand Mahindra', *The Economic Times*, April 9, 2019, last accessed 18th Feb, 2019. https://economictimes.indiatimes.com/magazines/panache/my-shareholders-pay-me-to-make-money-not-controversy-anand-mahindra/articleshow/63675170.cms

He spoke confidently of Ms Drew Faust, the Harvard president at the time, who had recommended that universities avoid making controversial statements or taking stands. Faust advised universities (and those involved with them) to focus not on stirring up a storm but encouraging meaningful conversation. Since universities enjoy an elevated status in society, they should be treated as safe houses that are catalysts for conversation, not breeding grounds for turmoil. Mr Mahindra surmised that fighting this battle would mean taking a stand that would benefit neither him nor his business.

2. Standing up for personal convictions

For many business houses in India, especially family-owned ones, the leader is the face of the empire. The said leader frequently finds himself attacked for personal statements and opinions, especially when they involve volatile subjects like patriotism or government projects that don't produce optimal results.

In February 2019, the Indian Railways inaugurated the Vande Bharat Express—India's first semi high-speed train. However, the train faltered on its maiden return voyage from Varanasi to Delhi. The BBC tweeted about the incident, mockingly reporting the news with an emoji depicting embarrassment. This wasn't a battle that Mr Anand Mahindra needed to take on for his business. But it was definitely one that stirred his personal belief and conviction in the work being done by the Indian government. He immediately reacted to the incident, posting this on his Twitter timeline:

'An emoji! Really @BBCWorld? Do you think you could have done a better job disguising your glee? The good thing is that it's this kind of attitude that makes us determined to do even better.'[53]

The public comment proved that he was willing to express displeasure without being afraid of antagonizing a prominent news channel. But it also spoke volumes of his desire to uphold personal beliefs—in this case, his patriotism. He has also been among the first major corporate leaders to publicly applaud any national achievements, as and when they are made.

CONTROL THE DISCUSSIONS YOU PARTICIPATE IN

There is one mega learning from Mr Anand Mahindra's approach to public battles: exercising caution. Managers and business leaders have responsibilities towards their stakeholders and cannot afford to let their impulses take complete control. Mr Mahindra is a public figure and reputed to be quite outspoken in day-to-day life. However, in making public statements and standing up for various issues, he exercises a measured, careful balance. First, he decides the topics to comment on using a detailed, ongoing process involving tremendous discipline. Second, he assesses the response he

---

[53] DNA online, accessed February 18, 2019. https://www.dnaindia.com/india/photo-gallery-this-attitude-makes-us-determined-to-do-better-anand-mahindra-s-response-to-bbc-tweet-emoji-on-train-18-breakdown-2720934/this-kind-of-attitude-makes-us-determined-to-do-even-better-2720940.

must issue to the chosen subjects that would get his point across but not give birth to controversy.

This two-step approach isn't as simple as it seems to be. For starters, the temptation to jump headlong into various discussions is immense in today's dynamic world. With business leaders like Mr Anand Mahindra, who is not only well known across the globe but whose opinions are also highly valued, the pressure to comment is significant. While this pressure sometimes comes in from the media, at other times, it is from the larger public. Not choosing to comment or abstaining from taking sides can be a risk too, as getting ignored is as big a slip as getting into hot water. But a business leader must let prudence and wisdom prevail.

A good rule of thumb here is to ensure that you *control* the issues or discussions you participate in and focus only on what is either important to you or enhances value for your shareholders. Leaders should use their energies for building their companies, not getting involved in frivolous controversies. This approach doesn't preach complete abandonment; it is a strategic, well-thought-out plan of choosing which battles to fight, instead of letting the battles—forever increasing in number—get the better of you with the sheer force of volume.

Another interesting lesson from Mr Mahindra is the smart way in which he balances his conversations. So, while most of his tweets cover various activities of the M&M Group, he also shows great wit and honesty in talking about personal topics. From hilarious misprints in the menu of a Chinese restaurant that served 'Delicious roasted husband'[54] to his experiences while working out[55], Mr Mahindra has established himself as a fascinating, well-rounded leader. A riveting personality and widespread interest in different topics is a good-to-have quality in a business leader of the modern generation.

---

[54]https://twitter.com/anandmahindra/status/ 1090479366235213824?ref_src=twsrc%5Etfw%7Ctwcamp%5E
[55]https://twitter.com/anandmahindra/status/9201182973115531008?lang=en

10
HONE YOUR LISTENING SKILLS

MOULD YOURSELF INTO A COMMITTED LISTENER WHO VALUES THE JUDGEMENT OF HIS PEOPLE. BE UNAFRAID OF DISSENT DURING DISCUSSIONS

For a business to be successful, the leader must focus on the development of soft skills just as much as skills considered 'core' to business, like understanding the sentiment of the market. A soft skill that has become an integral part of Mr Anand Mahindra's leadership style is a keen ability to listen. In his role as the group chairman, he invariably listens to the opinions of his team members and takes these into account before deciding on a plan of action. His motto of leadership is to cultivate an environment where people can express opinions—especially differing viewpoints—without having to watch over their backs with gnawing unease.

THE ANNUAL WAR ROOM

In 1997, when Mr Anand Mahindra took over as the MD of M&M, he started the culture of the annual war room. This was conceptualized to be a platform where strategies for each business of the group could be discussed periodically. The members participating in the war room—the Group Executive Board (GEB)—could then issue the final go/no go decision. The war room was also planned to be an avenue to take any other big-ticket decisions that could impact the individual companies in the M&M Group.

Since their inception, the annual war rooms have evolved into remarkably discerning platforms for discussion. Every year, the management teams from various group companies present their plans to the GEB. The GEB, in turn, accepts or challenges these plans after thorough discussions and announces its decisions. All major decisions have to be justified in the war room.

How are these annual war rooms different from any other budgetary or strategic meetings? Many members of M&M who have previously attended war rooms agree that the main difference lies in the easy, flowing dialogue and conversations. The participants find it comfortable to ask and answer questions—an advantage that can be attributed to the effort put in by Mr Mahindra. Even though he is the group chairman, he ensures to give all his team members equal respect and the freedom to communicate their ideas during the sessions. Many of his executives report that Mr Mahindra neither raises his voice during these discussions nor does he avoid answering questions addressed to him.[56]

Mr S.P. Shukla, who served as a former president of Group Strategy at M&M, recalls: 'In the strategy, operations and budget war rooms, I actually experienced how well Anand can encourage, promote and sustain dialogue between the business that is presenting and the corporate staff that is listening, brainstorming and contributing to the strategy.'[57]

Shukla adds that as the chairman, Mr Mahindra chose to facilitate conversations in a way that even the junior-most colleagues could speak their mind. The war room was a platform to show his leadership style.

One key aspect that has made the war rooms click over time is Mr Anand Mahindra's unwillingness to put his foot down on an issue before encouraging a discussion with his team of executives. Mr Shantanu Rege, the executive assistant to Mr Anand Mahindra from 2012 to 2016 and occasional attendee at these sessions, points out:[58]

> Whenever a question is posed, everyone wants to know what Anand is thinking. It's very easy for Anand to give an answer and for everybody else to fall in line and say, 'That's exactly what I was thinking.' But I love the way he

---

[56]V. Keshavdev, 'The Boss Anand Mahindra', *Outlook Business*, July 10, 2015, accessed November 2018. https://www.outlookbusiness.com/specials/the-boss/anand-mahindra-1258
[57]Ibid.
[58]Ibid.

does it—whenever a question is posed to him, he throws it back to the audience...

Mr Anand Mahindra thus ensured that his employee was made to feel like the smartest person around.

Mr Parag Shah, the managing partner of Mahindra Partners, concurs with this observation. He notes, 'In every meeting, in all probability, he (Mr Anand Mahindra) walks in knowing more about the subject than anyone else present. He has some indication of where he probably wants to be. But he still makes it a point to listen to everyone.'

UNIQUE STYLE OF QUESTIONING FOR OPTIMAL DECISION-MAKING

Both inside and outside the war room, Mr Anand Mahindra has developed a unique style of questioning. It is based on a meticulous combination of listening to his team and employing his assessment of the situation. According to Mr C.P. Gurnani, the CEO and MD of Tech Mahindra, this style of questioning is personal to Mr Mahindra in its indirect route to envisioning business concepts. Mr Gurnani cites an example to illustrate this approach:

> He (Mr Anand Mahindra) will never tell you that you should take a target 30 per cent higher. His questions would be in the form of what I call reflective conversations. He will say, 'If you were to grow your business exponentially, if you were planning a 10X

growth, what are the scenarios that you would look at?' Now, that is the kind of question where he has made you think, instead of being prescriptive.

In posing questions like these, Mr Mahindra succeeds in creating a collaborative environment where his team members get the opportunity to think and act together. Although the environment is shared, Mr Mahindra has a subtle solution for weeding out noise. His mantra, as described by Mr Gurnani, is to take decisions based 60 per cent on people's inputs and 40 per cent on his judgement. This is almost like an owner who bets on the jockey or the person who is going to execute, instead of the race or the turf. Mr Gurnani believes that this confidence he has in his people and his habit of carefully listening to them to weigh their judgement, influences the crucial 40 per cent of his assessment.

ENCOURAGING DISSENT TO BOOST PRODUCTIVITY

A noteworthy consequence of Mr Anand Mahindra's excellent listening skills is the growth of productive dissent within his team members. In an atmosphere where the leader promotes free thinking and does not veto disagreements, the employees find it easier to stand for what they believe in. This proved beneficial during the acquisitions of the Stokes Group, Jeco Holdings AG and Schöneweiss & Co. GmbH in the 2000s, led by Mr Luthra. It is reported that quite a few in the management were unconvinced about Mr Luthra's acquisition strategy. However, Mr Anand Mahindra, after hearing him out and deciding to side with him, did not withdraw his support. Mr Gurnani shares that this unflinching support must have derived from Mr Mahindra's firm conviction that Mr Luthra was going to create a billion-dollar conglomerate. After all, it did take time for multiple acquisitions to be integrated. Eventually, when the Mahindra-CIE deal happened in 2013, the shareholders benefited immensely.[59]

While some business leaders find it relatively easy to encourage discussions among their team members, even in an environment of dissent, they flounder when the disagreement is directed at them. Here, Mr Mahindra proves to possess a commendable advantage.

In the history of the M&M Group, there have been a few occasions when Mr Anand Mahindra has experienced widespread dissent or a strong argument against a view he has personally championed. There have been times when he has stalled the move in the middle of planning an acquisition after listening to contrary inputs from his employees. At times, some of these employees haven't even been from the core team. While he could have easily ignored such information and kept e-mails like this unread, he opted to listen.[60] The following two examples elucidate this lesson succinctly.

---

[59] V. Keshavdev, 'The Boss Anand Mahindra', *Outlook Business*, July 10, 2015, accessed November 2018. https://www.outlookbusiness.com/specials/the-boss/anand-mahindra-1258
[60] Ibid.

1. The wake of the 2008 financial crisis

During the 2008 financial crisis that shook the very foundation of the business world, several distressed assets came up in Dubai and parts of the U.S. Mr Anand Mahindra became interested in acquiring some of these assets. However, Ms Anita Arjundas, the CEO of the real estate sector at the time, advised against it. 'My view was that as an organization, we were not ready to go out of India and did not have sufficient management bandwidth to divert,' says Ms Arjundas.

Despite his eagerness to acquire the assets—many of which might have come in cheap—Mr Mahindra did as advised. Although he has developed an acute understanding of the business landscape in his long and eventful career, he genuinely believes in listening to his empowered team and not imposing his view.

2. The joint venture that could have been

In Chapter 6, we discussed how the M&M Group did not proceed with an automotive JV with a South African partner only because Mr Parthasarathy, the Group CFO, was uninterested in including M&M's tractors business in the clause. He maintained that the South African tractors market was too small and the costs for homologation and product development would be too high. Mr Anand Mahindra refused the JV in its present form on the grounds of a candid reason: he could not go against his team after having empowered them to make decisions.

DISSENT CAN BE REWARDED TO PROMOTE BUSINESS

Mr Anand Mahindra's single-minded focus on listening is more than just a humanitarian personality trait; it is part of his weaponry to protect and promote his business. By becoming an excellent listener who values the judgement of his employees, and creating an environment where his people can engage in open discussions, he has strengthened his business with the inimitable power of human intuition.

The concept of the annual war room is a simple yet effective way to draw out new ideas and offer managers a portal to test their ideas before execution. Since the managers have to present and defend their strategies in the war room, they have a lower likelihood of being blindsided or making errors in judgement due to an inadequately thought-out decision. This lets the organization trap and contain a misstep early in the process rather than jeopardizing the entire business on account of a half-baked strategy.

A lesson that managers must take home here is that of understanding when to be on the back foot. In the war room as also in his regular conduct in the group, Mr Anand Mahindra is mindful of how his statements could swing the mood of the entire room. He displays the wisdom and foresight to understand that voicing his decision first could alter the judgement of all his team members, tempting them to gravitate towards what 'the boss wants' instead of what they deem optimal. This is a fairly common bias seen in many management groups. The bias is also prevalent among the lower management layers who frequently go along with their seniors instead of expressing apprehensions.

To eliminate these risks, Mr Mahindra prefers to let his team members test their ideas and thoughts against each other instead of jumping in with what he finds best. In case the room comes up with a consensus contrary to that of his own, he is humble and sensible enough to encourage fearless conversations.

Finally, Mr Anand Mahindra's approach to team management also reinstates the need to encourage, not subdue disagreements. It is only when managers create processes and avenues congenial to frank discussions that healthy, constructive debates materialize. Many organizations have rather homogenous management groups with people from similar educational and social backgrounds. This escalates the risk of **group think** or tending to think exactly like the other group members. Eventually, the group comes up with a single view, with disconcerting or outlying aspects of the issue brushed under the carpet. A business that *likes* and *rewards* dissent will be likelier to benefit from the merits of differing viewpoints and nuances that come forth from arguments. Such an environment greatly promotes the tendency to think instead of blindly accepting.

11
HOMEWORK PRECEDES DECISIONS

TRUSTING IN YOUR TEAM IS IMPORTANT, BUT CONDUCTING YOUR OWN RESEARCH IS IMPERATIVE

Managers who believe in their teams often find a great source of comfort in how they can trust the judgement of their team members. After putting together an employee base of committed, qualified professionals, it should be possible to let these executives lead the research and come up with recommendations. But while it is certainly possible, it is not the approach that Mr Anand Mahindra champions without a significant rider: his own homework.

Conversations with several employees of the M&M Group indicate that Mr Mahindra is quick at grasping concepts. He is well known across the group for his intelligence and the uncanny ability to understand the depth of issues instantaneously. He uses this gift to gauge the temperament of his employees, for example, in the war room (Chapter 7), quietly sizing up different recommendations and letting his employees engage in meaningful discussions. However, these discussions are not the sole guideline on which he bases his decisions; his verdict ultimately rests on the observations of the research that he conducts in private.

THE SATYAM TAKEOVER

In 2009, the M&M Group was gearing up for the Satyam takeover. As we studied in Chapter 3, this was a time of major turbulence in Satyam, as they grappled with the financial scandal that threatened to eliminate all the goodwill they had earned over time. Mr Vineet Nayyar had already assured Mr Anand Mahindra that the takeover would be a wise decision. He had spoken with utter conviction of M&M's ability to manage the company and turn around its fortunes. While Mr Mahindra welcomed this opinion and gave it its due credit, he did not proceed with the takeover before conducting in-depth research on his own. In the days leading up to the deal, he undertook two activities:

1. **Roadshow:** Mr Anand Mahindra conducted a roadshow to understand customer perceptions towards Satyam. He personally took part in the roadshow to the U.S., along with his team. It turned out to be a welcome surprise. He observed that many of Satyam's

former customers were still positive about its future.

2. **Telephonic interactions:** While the reception to the roadshow pleasantly surprised Mr Anand Mahindra, it was not adequate. He decided to personally investigate the mood of Satyam's customers across the world. He picked up the phone and talked to customers, stakeholders and clients of Satyam, including Mr Kevin Turner, the CEO of Microsoft at that time and Mr Bill McDermott, the CEO of SAP. He also interacted with the top-tier managers at GE. The general opinion was overwhelmingly positive: despite the scandal, all of them stated that they were happy with Satyam's work and its people.

His research left him satisfied; it also validated the recommendation of Mr Nayyar. When he finally decided to go ahead with the takeover, Mr Anand Mahindra could feel at ease about his step, based solidly on ground research. As he confessed to *Forbes India* in 2013, the investigation made it pretty simple to arrive at a decision. He joked that for days, he was merely asking like the villain Gabbar Singh famously did in the blockbuster Bollywood film, *Sholay*, '*Kitne aadmi thhe?*' (How many good people were there at Satyam?).[61]

---

[61] Ashish Mishra and Cuckoo Paul, 'Anand Mahindra: The Federator', *Forbes India*, October 28, 2013, last accessed February 18, 2019, http://www.forbesindia.com/article/leaderhip-awards-2013/anand-mahindra-the-federator/36375/1

LEADERS MUST PREPARE FULLY EVEN IF THEY HAVE COMPETENT TEAMS

The learning from this chapter is compact but irreplaceable—it is a lesson that can be the making or undoing of your business. Mr Anand Mahindra's insistence on conducting due diligence and keeping himself fully prepared highlights the importance of homework. His detail-oriented methodology of basing all decisions on personally completed homework has proved to be a major asset for his business. All his decisions stem from foolproof preparation and complete information—a winning amalgam that limits the scope for mistakes.

There is another reason why Mr Anand Mahindra stresses the need to get your hands dirty in the field, even when a group of qualified and competent professionals is available to do the same; he believes that it is a good practice of governance. The standard procedure that Mr Mahindra follows is to employ his listening skills, consider everyone's viewpoints, conduct research at his end, and finally, take the matter to the board. Involving his personal assessment so completely in every major decision expresses his willingness to be questioned and have his ideas examined. During the Satyam deal, for instance, Mr Anand Mahindra sought the approval of Mr Keshub Mahindra. His uncle, in turn, insisted that the decision should be taken to the M&M Board for approval. It was the standard practice to make decisions in consultation with the board, and no situation was beyond or beneath implementing this important process of transparent governance.

This approach becomes especially praiseworthy when you observe the contrast it holds with many other family-run businesses. It is quite common with family business promoters to choose to ignore the board and run the company like their fiefdom. There is limited, if any, respect for the shareholders' interests. But the M&M Group has maintained a strict adherence to proper governance.

12

GROW BY ACQUISITION

EXPLORE THE PATH OF TAKEOVERS AND INTERNATIONAL EXPANSION FOR GROWTH, WHILE CONSISTENTLY STRENGTHENING THE CORE OF YOUR BUSINESS

In the Indian business landscape, most business houses adopt one of two means for growth: choosing to set up a new company in an allied or previously unexplored sector, or acquiring an existing company and integrating it into the fold. The M&M Group has majorly relied on the latter strategy, preferring to grow by acquisition. Let us explore the nuances of this strategy and how the group has managed to adapt it to their advantage.

ESTABLISHING A LEAD IN THE TRACTORS INDUSTRY

M&M started manufacturing agricultural vehicles in 1962, during the time of the Licence Raj in India. It soon became a leading player in the domestic market, which was a direct benefit of the prevailing regime that limited the number of licences issued to competing players in a sector. The competition was marginal, and M&M had a low-pressure environment in which to grow. In the 1990s, the Indian economy opened up with the ushering in of liberalization. This led to an almost immediate boom in the rural economy, also leading to increased sales for M&M.

M&M rode this boom brilliantly, engaging in rapid expansion by taking over Punjab Tractors, a rival company, in 2007. This step helped M&M get a 40 per cent share of the total market.

Ever since that initial, highly fruitful acquisition, M&M has been deepening its footprint in the tractors sector. From 2004 to 2008, the group signed two JVs in China—with the Yueda Group and the Jiangling Tractor Company. It also increased its exports to other developing countries like India in a bid to expand its international footprint.

Mr Anand Mahindra and his team have constantly been looking for acquisitions abroad to cement the group's international reputation and standing. In 2012, M&M overtook John Deere, a tractor manufacturer from Illinois, U.S., to become the world's largest tractor producer by volume.

STEERING STRATEGIC ACQUISITIONS IN THE CARS SECTOR

After tractors, another sector of great significance for M&M is that of two-wheelers. Here too, the group has made calculated acquisitions to entrench its footprint.

1. Reva

In 2010, M&M took over Reva, an electric vehicle manufacturer based in Bengaluru, India. It paid ₹150 crore for the ingenious technology. Mr Pawan Goenka felt that while Reva had a well-regarded, useful product, along with superior technology and ambitious plans, it lacked the resources to make the most of these assets. Around this time, the Government of India also announced tax breaks for electric vehicles. This helped guarantee a good beginning for the takeover.

2. SsangYong

In January 2009, SsangYong, the South Korean automobile manufacturer, filed for bankruptcy. SsangYong's sales had crashed due to high fuel prices and rising emission standards in the countries to which it had previously exported its cars. The global financial crisis had borne down heavily on the company, and it found itself unable to bear these challenges. The rampant labour strikes in the company only made things worse.

When M&M declared its intentions to acquire SsangYong, the market did not respond favourably. There was an instant drop in its stock prices. Who would want to connect with a failing company and get tarred by association? But M&M had concrete reasons for being interested in this acquisition. SsangYong had strong capabilities in technology that could complement M&M's competence in financing, sourcing and marketing. Mr Pawan Goenka, the president of the automotive and farm equipment sector at the time, strongly felt that the acquisition would also help M&M introduce a premium SUV portfolio in the Indian market.[62] It would provide a growth avenue for the ailing SsangYong, but more importantly, it would strengthen M&M's dominant position in the utility vehicle (UV) segment.

M&M participated in the bidding along with seven other prospective buyers, including the Pawan Ruia Group, Renault-Nissan, a private equity firm called Seoul Invest, and the Young An Hat Co. Ltd. from South Korea.

Mr Anand Mahindra's decision to acquire SsangYong did not go down well with many of the investors. Some of them observed how the takeover of an international auto company frequently ran into problems, citing the previous acquisition of JLR by Tata Motors. After the Tata Group had finalized the deal (in 2008), the company remained burdened with debt for a long time. It was several tiresome years before the JLR operations started making profits. What if the proposed SsangYong takeover led to a similar situation?

---

[62]'Mahindra buys 70% in SsangYong', *Business Standard*, January 20, 2013. Accessed November 10, 2018. https://www.business-standard.com/article/companies/mahindra-buys-70-in-ssangyong-110112400046_1.html

Interestingly, SsangYong did its best to facilitate the deal. The transaction was smooth and free of debt. The company also trimmed the workforce before M&M took over, reducing the pressure on the human resources team to undertake organizational integration. M&M paid a purchase price of $463 million (₹2,100 crore) for a 70 per cent stake. This was at a 60 per cent discount of what Shanghai Automotive Industry Corporation (SAIC), the Chinese owner company, had paid back in 2004.[63]

Post the takeover, Mr Anand Mahindra knew that he had to win over the unions and the investors. Only when his people worked in synergy for the turnaround of the newly acquired company would the results be quick. He rolled out the following initiatives to improve the post-acquisition situation and create the synergies he wanted to see:

- **Trimming the management:** M&M appointed only six people in the management team of SsangYong. The only Indian among the top executives was Mr Dilip Sundaram, the CFO. The operations were headed by

---

[63]M.G. Arun, 'Mahindra and Mahindra: Driving the change in India's automotive industry', *India Today*, August 11, 2017, accessed November 10, 2018. https://www.indiatoday.in/magazine/cover-story/story/20170821-mahindra-mahindra-car-company-anand-mahindra-automotive-industry-muv-suv-segment-1028902-2017-08-11

Kushan Mitra, 'We will create a system that is impregnable', *Business Today*, September 13, 2011, Accessed November 8, 2018, https://www.businesstoday.in/opinion/interviews/anand-mahindra-satyam-rise/story/18639.html.

Mr Yoo-Il Lee from South Korea.

- **Establishing the Synergy Council:** Mr Mahindra set in place a council comprising the senior management from both the companies. This council would work to ensure focus and delivery of synergies between the two companies, concentrating on aspects like global procurement, new car development and business strategies to penetrate international markets.
- **Following a five-point agenda:** Finally, M&M proposed an agenda for SsangYong to regain its lost ground and become profitable. The action items included strengthening the product pipeline, harnessing synergies between the two companies, investing in the SsangYong brand, building human resources and focusing on financial stability.[64]
- **Developing new products:** At the time of the takeover, SsangYong manufactured approximately 1,20,000 vehicles with over 65 per cent of them exported. M&M decided to invest resources in bringing in freshness within the company. In 2013, M&M spent $900 million in developing new products for SsangYong. It also launched Tivoli, its first compact SUV, at the Shanghai Auto Show in 2015.
- **Setting up new plants:** In November 2017, M&M announced the setting up of a Detroit-based plant with

---

[64]Mahindra website, accessed November 2018, http://www.mahindra.com/news-room/press-release/1300159661

an investment of $230 million. This would be Detroit's first automotive production facility in twenty-five years. Year 2018 onwards, the plant started work on producing off-road and work vehicles.[65] M&M already had many tractor assembly plants all over the U.S. and as of 2017, employed about 3,000 workers in its global workforce of more than 200,000. The Auburn plant was small, with a technical centre and two related operations employing a total of 270 people. Through the new plant, M&M expected to add another 400 jobs in Detroit by 2020. The group also planned to invest another $600 million in the area.

The above steps reaped rewarding results. Tivoli became an immediate hit and went on to become a major success for the group. In 2016, the sales volume of the vehicle increased to 1,55,844 units—the highest reported by the company since 2002.[66] The popularity of the new product steadily helped SsangYong. By 2017, the company had achieved continuous growth for over eight straight years in domestic sales. It also

---

[65]Bill Vlasic, 'Indian Automaker's Plant is Latest sign of Detroit comeback, *The New York Times*, November 20, 2017. Accessed November 10, 2018. https://www.nytimes.com/2017/11/20/business/detroit-indian-automaker.html?login=email&auth=login-email

[66]Malyaban Ghosh, 'Mahindra-owned SsangYong slips back into losses in 2017', Livemint, February 22, 2018. Accessed November 10, 2018. https://www.livemint.com/Companies/puoSNkpKpcA7hUJOB4CujI/Mahindraowned-SsangYong-slips-back-into-losses-in-2017.html

benefitted from the successful launch of Rexton—another high-end SUV.[67]

The setting up of the Detroit plant proved to be a winning strategy adopted by M&M. Mr Anand Mahindra wanted his group to be a major part of the U.S. markets. Detroit—also known as the Motor City in the U.S.—was the logical spot to centre his attention. This was the location of choice for many major car manufacturers. It also had a sizeable concentration of talent and suppliers, which made it easy for M&M to tap into the auto industry's research and development activities.[68]

3. Pininfarina

In December 2015, M&M purchased Pininfarina, an Italian design and engineering firm, for a total investment of $185 million. This Italian design house was the legendary styling brand behind luxury cars by Ferrari, Alfa Romeo and Peugeot, among others.[69]

---

[67] Malyaban Ghosh, 'Mahindra-owned SsangYong slips back into losses in 2017', Livemint, February 22, 2018. Accessed November 10, 2018. https://www.livemint.com/Companies/puoSNkpKpcA7hUJOB4CujI/Mahindraowned-SsangYong-slipsback-into-losses-in-2017.html

[68] Pavan Lall, 'Anand Mahindra, adventure capitalist', *Fortune India*, December 5, 2010. Accessed November 11, 2018. https://www.fortuneindia.com/people/anand-mahindra-adventure-capitalist/101132

[69] Jeremy Korzeniewski, 'Mahindra buys Pininfarina for $28 million,' Online Blog, accessed November 8, 2018, https://www.autoblog.com/2015/12/14/mahindra-buys-pininfarina-28million/

Mr Anand Mahindra's compelling reason behind this acquisition was to enhance the design capabilities of the entire M&M Group. While explaining the reasons for this takeover in a press release, he said that the customers were becoming increasingly design sensitive, and product design would greatly influence customer experiences and choices in the future. Pininfarina's exceptional design skills were legendary and would become a key asset for the acquirer (in this case, Tech Mahindra).[70]

There was another associated advantage of the acquisition: it would give Tech Mahindra an early foothold in the automotive vertical. Pininfarina had a focused presence in Italy, Germany, the U.S. and China—countries that were traditional automotive strongholds—and the acquisition would help Tech Mahindra reap the benefits.

In all these acquisitions, it is worth noting that M&M also paid attention to the modus operandi. So, when it was deemed optimal, Mr Anand Mahindra roped in private equity players for materializing the acquisitions. For instance, M&M partnered with ICICI Venture for the purchase of Metalcastello, an Italian auto component company. For acquiring GippsAero, the Australian aeroplane maker, it collaborated with Kotak Private Equity.

On several occasions, M&M also faced setbacks during

---

[70] Mahindra Press Release, "Pininfarina becomes the latest jewel in Tech Mahindra Crown," December 12, 2015, accessed March 12, 2019, https://www.techmahindra.com/media/press_releases/Pininfarina-becomes-the-latest-jewel-in-TechMahindra-crown.aspx

their acquisition strategy. Study the following examples:

1. Aston Martin

In 2012, M&M bid for Aston Martin, the British sports car maker. Aston Martin had gained immense fame for being associated with James Bond, the fictional spy. But the Kuwaiti owners of Aston Martin were looking for new investments. Eventually, M&M lost the bid to Investindustrial, an Italian private equity fund.

2. Jaguar Land Rover

As we discussed in Chapter 8, M&M participated in the bidding for JLR, competing against the Tata Group. But it preferred to step back and accept the loss of the bid to the Tatas after Mr Anand Mahindra assessed that the price being asked was much heftier than his group could risk paying.

It is essential to note here that Mr Mahindra, while enthusiastic about achieving growth through acquisition, knew when to step back and call off a deal if it did not measure up to his risk assessment framework.

Mr Anand Mahindra understands and admits that the acquisition strategy doesn't come without its failings. The biggest challenge he has faced is successfully integrating the takeovers into the group—an activity that requires a lot of time and effort. While he claims that he enjoys this experience, he also knows how to address it like a professional. The M&M Group has steered a turnaround in many of the companies they have taken over, and the exercise is a challenging but rewarding one. During the integration of the takeovers, Mr Anand Mahindra has endeavoured to exercise patience and maintain a realistic, practical approach. He draws reassurance from a simple plan of giving every integration process his best shot and then following a principle of wait-and-watch to see the results of his actions. This is infinitely preferable compared to rushing into things and expecting grand results overnight.

PIONEERING NEW VENTURES

Balancing the group's strategy of acquisition and growth by entering JVs, is Mr Anand Mahindra's rollout of original, independent enterprises. Let us review two examples.

1. Entering the defence sector

In 2009, M&M developed the Marksman, an urban patrol vehicle based on Scorpio. It was launched with an eye on the defence sector in India. He has also started the Mahindra Land Defence Systems, a JV with British Aerospace, aspiring to get a 20 per cent share of the $100 billion defence market in the near future.[71]

2. Investing in electric scooters

Inspired by the successful investment in Reva's electric vehicles, M&M, in 2016, invested in Scoots Networks, an American

---

[71] Kushan Mitra, 'Top Gun', *Business Today*, October 2, 2011, accessed October 10, 2018. https://www.businesstoday.in/magazine/cover-story/anand-mahindra-mandm-company-acquisitions/story/18656.html

company that provides electric scooters. The investment was made through Mahindra Partners, its venture arm. Scoots, headquartered in San Francisco, had been engaged in the business of providing electric mobility since 2012. Mr Anand Mahindra is also working on kick-starting Mahindra Two Wheelers—renamed from its former identity of Kinetic and Mahindra Motorcycles.

TAKEAWAY

The business history of M&M hints at the utility of an acquisition-led growth strategy. The group has used acquisitions at a reasonable valuation to attain faster growth. In fact, some statistics report that Mr Anand Mahindra has made as many as thirty-five acquisitions as of 2013![72] The pace has been maintained ever since.

The industrialist in Mr Mahindra understands the need to protect the core business, amidst the raging need for growth and diversification. He has effectively used available opportunities to strengthen M&M's market share in tractors. He has also worked towards improving the group's competitiveness in the auto sector. Protecting and continually strengthening the core industry is important to keep a company sustainable and

---

[72]Shally Seth Mohile and Deepti Chaudhary, 'Mahindra shifts from M&As to stitching up global alliances,' Livemint, June 17, 2013, accessed March 12, 2019. https://www.livemint.com/Industry/9PP9i0DTP97BHFynTPDSLK/Mahindra-shifts-from-MAs-to-stitching-up-global-alliances.html

provide valuable cash flows for future investments.

Where some other companies could become overly euphoric in the wake of successes brought on by acquisitions, thereby losing sight of the present, Mr Anand Mahindra has consistently prioritized what he believes is the mainstay of his business. In their bid to increase profits, business leaders must remember where these profits come from at that time; it would never do to look only in the direction of the future.

A key takeaway from this chapter is a lesson that every business aspirant—from an MBA student to an entrepreneur—needs to keep close to his or her heart. Mr Anand Mahindra's business strategy for growth is based on **risk mitigation**, or the methods used by a company to reduce the risk in any given scenario. M&M used two methods during acquisitions to achieve this:

1. Being cautious when pursuing acquisitions, especially those perceived to be high-risk or those with high valuations and intense demands for integration
2. Stepping down from a pursuit when judgement advises it

The group's decision to drop out of the JLR race is a strong example of the second method; the leader didn't find it lucrative to vie with the Tatas for the deal, as the former's deeper pockets lent them an advantage that M&M lacked.

The final takeaway from this chapter is the balance that Mr Anand Mahindra has managed to achieve in being aggressive towards acquisitions but realistic and practical towards their outcomes. He realizes the challenges of integrating the newly acquired companies within the group and does not pressure his team to showcase results until these challenges have been resolved. Being conservative in his expectations has helped him achieve results that stem from strategic structural and business-level changes effected in the acquired company. They don't emanate from patchwork efforts aimed at satisfying a business leader who likes to count his proverbial chickens before they hatch.

Mr Anand Mahindra has, undoubtedly, adapted the acquisition strategy to his group's advantage. He remains humble and confident at the same time, observing that it is an ongoing effort. Mr Ulhas N. Yargop, President, IT sector, describes the guiding principle at work astutely: 'In everything the Mahindra Group does, we are specialists in something. The rationale is to be No. 1 in that specialisation.'[73]

At M&M, the commitment to specializing in a segment runs through all the activities of the group—from the UVs in automobiles, and tractors in agricultural products, to holiday resorts (Club Mahindra).[74]

---

[73]Kunal N. Talgeri, 'Inside the Merger!' *Fortune India*, December 5, 2012, last accessed February 18, 2019. https://www.fortuneindia.com/technology/inside-the-merger/100760

[74]Ibid.

13
INVEST WITH AN EYE ON THE FUTURE

INVEST IN TOMORROW'S TECHNOLOGIES WHILE THE PRESENT CORE BUSINESS IS STILL STRONG

It is natural for business houses to make investments to fuel their growth; what doesn't come as naturally to many businesses is investing in future-oriented projects. While investments in sectors that show profitable returns in the present times offer a sense of solace, it is riskier and requires greater foresight to spend on products and technologies that may be nascent at present but possess immense potential. Mr Anand Mahindra's investment style for the M&M Group has been directed at the future with the goal of leapfrogging the competition.

THE ELECTRIC VEHICLE BET

In 2018, *Fortune India* published a report on Mr Anand Mahindra, applauding the uncanny foresight and vision in his forecast of the rise of battery-powered vehicles or electric vehicles (EVs) in India.[75] The editorial stated that Mr Mahindra possessed the three key attributes that make entrepreneurs successful: grit, instinct and the ability to undertake course corrections whenever needed. The glowing report was based on an incredible decision Mr Anand Mahindra had made to invest in the sector of EVs. It had been at a time when few competitors were exploring something so nascent and fledgling, but Mr Mahindra foresaw that the sector had a promising future. He bet that the rising pollution due to vehicular emissions in most Indian cities would raise the demand for EVs in India. A research report published by Morgan Stanley Research in May 2017 agreed with his judgement, predicting that EVs could become a $60 billion opportunity for India in the next decade.

In 2010, Mr Anand Mahindra steered M&M to the position of the first leading player in this space by buying out Reva Electric, an electric vehicle company owned by Mr Chetan Maini. He renamed it Mahindra Electric (ME) and designated Mr Pawan Goenka as the chairman. Mr Mahindra was driven by three primary reasons for buying out Reva:

---

[75]Sourav Majumdar, 'Mahindra's electric bet', *Fortune India*, July 11, 2018, accessed November 10, 2018. https://www.fortuneindia.com/macro/mahindras-electric-bet/102122

1. The need to offer less-polluting vehicles in India;
2. The expectations that battery prices would crash, thus making EVs affordable;
3. The opportunity to become leaders in the electric vehicle technology and components segment.

He has bet big on this industry and made elaborate strategic moves, expecting it to be a space where M&M can be the leader as well as the source of technology and components.

Since the acquisition, M&M has faced quite a bit of competition in the EVs sector in India. Comparable EVs made by Tesla, Nissan, Toyota and General Motors exist. Tesla's initial model—the Roadster—debuted in 2008 at $109,000. In 2010, Nissan launched the Leaf—an all-electric, battery-operated car. General Motors also launched a comparable product in the same year—a hybrid called the Volt. The Volt used a gasoline engine to charge the battery for additional mileage. Finally, Toyota's hybrid car—the Prius—also grew to become popular; however, this battery-operated vehicle was heavily subsidized under state government subsidies.

By comparison, Reva was priced at around ₹2.5 lakh—much lower than most of the contemporaries. Even so, it sold only a few hundred cars annually. Although the maintenance costs were less and the rides promised to be stress-free, Reva seemed only mildly popular with the audience.

In 2013, Mahindra launched the e20, a mainstream-looking electric car. It was priced at ₹6.5 lakh. The e20 did not do well either, once again selling only about a hundred cars annually. Over the next five years, Reva's fortunes did not change. This was a setback for M&M, especially since the company had invested in a futuristic factory with great hopes and also overhauled the product design. M&M had even undertaken an extensive rebranding of the product.

It was then that Mr Anand Mahindra realized where the group had been faltering: the battle in the EV sector could not be waged promisingly in the individual ownership markets; it had to be fought in the institutional market. Most of the individual buyers were unimpressed by the 'coolness factor' of driving an EV. They were also unsure of the government's ability to provide sufficient charging points across different cities in India.

After wrapping his thoughts around the situation and realising the need for a course correction, Mr Mahindra moved quickly. In 2017, he forged a partnership with Ola, the popular fleet operator. Ola announced that it would lease hundred EVs from ME. M&M also signed on the dotted line with Lithium, a transportation company that ran on clean energy. Lithium required a competent EV with a range of 120–50 km, which could service its needs for a fleet car.

Alongside, Mr Mahindra entered into partnerships with bulk purchasers like Energy Efficiency Services Ltd (ESSL) in the public sector. ESSL is a JV of the public sector units under India's Ministry of Power. It includes the National Thermal Power Corporation Limited (NTPC), the Power Finance Corporation, the Rural Electrification Corporation and the Power Grid Corporation. The agreement entailed that ESSL would purchase EVs by tender, and distribute them to various government departments. This would be an effort to replace the existing diesel and petrol vehicles.[76] Surprisingly, the first of these tenders was won by Tata Motors, even though it was a surprise entrant. The conscious move towards environmentally efficient vehicles seems well-thought-out; in 2017, Tony Seba, a Stanford economist, predicted that all sales of diesel and petrol cars would cease by 2030![77]

Indeed, the strategic shift proved to be a step in the right direction for M&M. Soon, the group started noticing an uptick in the demand for its EVs. Meru, another aggregator like Ola, initiated a pilot project in Hyderabad with electric cars leased from M&M. Baghirathi, a Bengaluru-based, twenty-year-old car-hire company with a fleet of 3,000 conventional fuel cars, placed an order for 1,000 ME cars. Zoomcar, a company that offers self-drive cars on hire, also began to provide cars by ME in Mumbai.

Mr Mahesh Babu, the CEO of ME as of 2019, sums up M&M's approach in the EV sector brilliantly.[78] He says that

---

[76]Prerna Lidhoo, 'EESL floats second tender for acquiring 10,000 EVs', *Fortune India*, March 10, 2018, https://www.fortuneindia.com/macro/eesl-floats-second-tender-for-acquiring-10000-evs/101658

[77]CarAndBike Team, 'Petrol And Diesel Cars Will Vanish In 8 Years: Study', *NDTV Auto*, May 21, 2017, accessed March 2, 2019 https://auto.ndtv.com/news/petrol-and-diesel-cars-will-vanish-in-8-years-study-1696406

[78]Kushan Mitra, 'Top Gun', *Business Today*, October 2, 2011. Accessed October 10, 2018. https://www.businesstoday.in/magazine/cover-story/anand-mahindra-mandm-company-acquisitions/story/18656.html

the group has decided to use its investment not to create an aspirational product (like Tesla), but to become a mass-market brand with a product that can solve societal problems in India.

PURSUING GREATER PUBLIC GOOD

M&M's pursuit of the EV sector highlights the group's eagerness to accrue benefits for the entire ecosystem, including the country at large. The benefits of EVs would apply to the whole country and therefore, would become a line of business that furthers profits for its investors as well as contributes to public and environmental betterment.

Mr Pawan Goenka once stated in an article published in *Fortune*, with respect to EVs: when M&M as a group loses market share to other players, it would mean that the entire EV space is growing.[79] This played out in the case of the petrol SUV space where Mahindra lost its leadership position to competitors like Maruti, Hyundai and Ford. However, in the case of EVs, the decision went beyond the hazard of losing market share—it threatened the company's future. The group's decision to pursue growth in the sector, despite the risks, reveals its interests in contributing to social welfare.

---

[79]Surendar T., 'M&M's EV bet: All charged up and not sure where to go', *Fortune India* online, August 1, 2018, accessed March 12, 2019. https://www.fortuneindia.com/enterprise/mahindra-mahindra-mm-ev-bet-all-charged-up-and-not-sure-where-to-go/102226

FUTURE ORIENTATION AND CONSTANT EXPERIMENTATION

Mr Anand Mahindra has maintained a close watch on the core business of his group and initiated investments that strengthen it for challenges to come. However, his investment focus has also spread to new businesses that branch away from the core business of M&M. For instance, during the late 1990s to the late 2000s, he launched a used-car portal (Mahindra First), a technology-led logistics business (Mahindra Logistics) and a venture for manufacturing boats (Mahindra Marine). He has also led the group into diverse areas, including hospitality, finance and software. As of 2011, these new areas of investment contributed to over 40 per cent of the group's valuation.

In an interview with *Harvard Business Review*, Mr Anand Mahindra outlined his ambition for the group:[80]

> My aspiration is that M&M become one of the most customer-centric organizations in the world. If we focus on understanding our customers, we will be able to develop customer-centric innovations. By that, I don't mean we should only ask customers for product ideas; I'm aware, of course, that Sony would have never developed the Walkman if it had listened solely to its customers.

---

[80] Thomas Stewart and Anand Raman, 'Finding a Higher Gear', *Harvard Business Review*, July-August 2008, accessed November 2018. https://hbr.org/2008/07/finding-a-higher-gear

He adds that he wants to follow the example of design firm IDEO, where consultants observe a customer vacuum the floor so that they can ideate what the product should do and what it should look like.

Mr Mahindra backed this lofty ambition with action. In the mid-1990s, he approved the development of a new concept car—the Scorpio (Chapter 16), even though the group lacked the financial resources that his Western competitors possessed. This new SUV came in at a total cost of $120 million—about one-fifth of what other auto companies would spend on a comparable project. It was perhaps the biggest gamble of Mr Anand Mahindra's career so far. But instead of costing him his job, it went on to win numerous prestigious awards and also established the group as a serious global competitor in the automotive market.

PLAN AHEAD FOR FUTURISTIC INVESTMENTS

Mr Anand Mahindra has consistently displayed a knack for making investments that have the potential to reap rewards in the near future. His experiences have helped him develop the visionary thinking to forecast where the market is headed and work towards reaching there before competitors. Such forecasting, and the associated risks it entails of patiently waiting for the future to play out, requires a great deal of courage. Mr Anand Mahindra has demonstrated this ability in his investment in the EV sector—a step taken much in advance of competitors and with a vision to shape the future.

His buyout of Reva helped M&M become the first major player in the segment.

Futuristic investments have terrific potential for a business. But to implement them with minimal risk of failure, the business leader must have the ability to understand the market (in this case, the automobile market) and be willing to work patiently towards his or her goals. It is an approach that can work only when paired with a measured outlook that envisions the company as a significant player for tomorrow—whether in the sectors of SUVs, electric vehicles, solar technology or IT.

14

CREATE ONE IDENTITY

UNITE YOUR EMPLOYEES, ACQUISITIONS AND OTHER ASSETS UNDER A COMMON IDENTITY; IT IS THE ONLY MANTRA TO ENSURE A CONCERTED AND PRODUCTIVE EFFORT

In 2009, Mr Scott Goodson, the founder of an advertising agency called Strawberry Frog, came to meet Mr Anand Mahindra in Mumbai. At the time, Strawberry Frog had an interesting clientele; one of their clients was Global Vehicles, the U.S. distributor of M&M's Scorpio. Mr Goodson's trip to India was intended to understand the M&M Group better. He also wanted to explore the core purpose of the group.

Mr Goodson's meetings with Mr Mahindra, however, were contrary to what either gentleman may have expected. The former had this to say about the company: the managers at M&M believed that they were working for a higher purpose, but they were unable to articulate what it was. It was possible, he announced rather boldly, that Mr Anand Mahindra had himself not understood the kind of company he was running.

While Mr Goodson may have been somewhat blunt in his observations, what he said resonated to an extent with Mr Anand Mahindra. M&M had grown rapidly in a relatively short period, but the growth had been primarily by acquisitions. Over time, the group had evolved to have multiple nationalities; hundreds of people of Korean, German, American and Chinese origin worked for the group. It wasn't true that the group lacked an articulated core purpose; Mr Anand Mahindra operated by the loosely defined motto of 'Indians are second to none'. But after his meeting with Mr Goodman, he assessed that this was a dated motto that warranted a change if M&M had to continue succeeding on a global stage. The old slogan had been framed at the time of India's independence and failed to capture the changing, multinational vibe that had since developed in the company.

THE RISE CAMPAIGN: IN PURSUIT OF A COMMON IDENTITY

The brand campaign that brought about a monumental change in the perception of the M&M Group—the Rise Campaign—was launched in 2011. In Goodson's meetings with Mr Anand Mahindra, where the former had made it clear that M&M needed to develop *one* identity, he hit upon an insight: all consumers, both current and prospective, wanted to shape their destiny. Associating with a company enabled them to do this. However, consumers looked for companies they could trust, and whose integrity and ideals they could believe in. Only those consumers who trusted a company would be willing to become stakeholders, even though they were only consumers.

After months of research and interviews with the stakeholders, the M&M Group came up with the Rise Campaign. It was based on three core principles:

1. Accept no limits;
2. Think alternatively;
3. Drive positive change.

The Rise Campaign was kick-started through a transformation within the M&M Group, with all the employees internalizing the motto and asking themselves one crucial question: how would they enable people to rise?

In 2011, when the campaign was launched, the group comprised over 1,20,000 people, of which over 65,000–70,000 worked in the IT business. It was a huge, widespread employee base that could work optimally only when connected through a common purpose. This is precisely what this campaign aimed at achieving. The campaign became especially useful and started showing exceptional results after the Satyam collapse in 2009, when M&M took over the same to form the company Mahindra-Satyam (see Chapter 12). This was also the time when M&M took over Reva in India and SsangYong in Korea. The Rise Campaign helped to integrate the people within the group and granted them a common sense of identity.

Historically, the Rise Campaign has been one of the most successful corporate campaigns in India. It was eagerly accepted by the employees and actively propagated on social media.[81] The campaign for the U.S. launch, however, was shelved because of legal issues with Global Vehicles, and the U.S. advertisements were never made public.

BRANDING SHOULD IMPLY A COLLECTIVE IDENTITY

Mr Anand Mahindra is a business leader who operates by balance. While ardently patriotic and committed to the cause of development in India, he knows when it is imperative to achieve equilibrium between looking homewards and charting international waters. While the roots of the M&M Group were in India, the scope eventually increased to different countries of the world. Once the group had thus expanded, its India-focused motto could prove to be restrictive and out of context. The rebranding undertaken by Mr Mahindra aspired to make the group more inclusive and relevant to its global ambitions. This rebranding exercise would also unify the employees and help them develop a shared vision, even if they worked at a worldwide scale from remote locations across the globe.

Business leaders—especially those who run large organizations—must implement a collective identity across

---

[81] Kushan Mitra, 'We will create a system that is impregnable', *Business Today*, September 13, 2011, Accessed November 8, 2018, https://www.businesstoday.in/opinion/interviews/anand-mahindra-satyam-rise/story/18639.html.

their business. This becomes even more critical if the business adopts growth by acquisition as its primary expansion vehicle. In the absence of a unifying identity, the acquired company and its people could easily feel lost or disparate, unable to align themselves with the new company's vision. Such acquisitions—while being assets in their own right—would never develop teams willing to rally around a theme or understand what needed to be done for collaborative work.

15

JOINT VENTURES NEVER GO OUT OF STYLE

ENTER INTO JOINT VENTURES WITH GUSTO AND A CLEARLY DEFINED OBJECTIVE; BE CONFIDENT OF YOUR ABILITY TO MAKE THEM WORK

For the M&M Group, JVs have always been the mainstay. Mr Anand Mahindra has entered into such deals across sectors, with variable success. But while not all JVs have been successful, he has certainly learnt an important lesson from this approach. He believes that a business leader must understand the probability of success of a JV at the outset and that this ratio is fairly straightforward—50:50. While signing on the dotted line, Mr Mahindra keeps in mind that 50 per cent of the deals may not work and require commitment from both parties to turn the situation around. No JV is worth its salt if the partners are unwilling to evaluate its merits and commit to an action plan for its success.

In selecting the JVs to pursue, Mr Mahindra analyses if they fulfil any (or all) of these key objectives:

- Become a tool for growth;
- Be a point of entry into a sector or market;
- Help overcome barriers;
- Prove useful for learning.

As time has passed, the M&M Group has matured in its treatment of JVs. It enters JVs with a clear understanding of what each party would derive from the deal and where this benefit stands in the larger scheme of the business.

JOINT VENTURES IN THE AUTO SECTOR

The first JV of the M&M Group was with the Ford Motor Company of the U.S., back in 1995. Through this JV, Mr Anand Mahindra expected to gain management expertise and, more critically, access to superior technology. However, the first product of this JV—the Escort car—flopped, and the venture fizzled out.

Subsequently, M&M entered into a spate of other JVs in the auto sector. But they did not play out well either. The group's JV with the U.S.-based Navistar International was constantly plagued by delays in rolling out medium and heavy commercial vehicles. There was stiff competition from local, low-cost rivals such as Asia Motor Works Limited, a large automobile manufacturer in India, and the JV never managed to rise above it. M&M's JV with Renault, which it entered into in 2005, also produced only limited success. The mid-sized sedan, Logan, failed to take off, and the remaining cars, which were being sold under the brand Verito, did not achieve for Renault the audience segment it was trying to win. The partners parted ways after four years.[82]

On the surface, it seems as if M&M has had a dismal experience as far as JVs in the auto sector are concerned. However, if you dig deep, it becomes clear that many of the eventual successes of the M&M Group were founded in the learning and benefits derived from these early partnerships.

Mr Anand Mahindra frequently cites the example of the JV with Ford—a deal he had signed with clear plans and objectives. When M&M was working on Scorpio, the vehicle that continues to be one of the group's biggest successes, he insisted that the car be initially manufactured at Nashik. The rationale was simple: Mr Mahindra wanted the team that had

---

[82] MG Arun, 'Mahindra and Mahindra: Driving the change in India's automotive industry', *India Today*, August 11, 2017, accessed November 10, 2018. https://www.indiatoday.in/magazine/cover-story/story/20170821-mahindra-mahindra-car-company-anand-mahindra-automotive-industry-muv-suv-segment-1028902-2017-08-11;
Kushan Mitra, 'We will create a system that is impregnable', *Business Today*, September 13, 2011, Accessed November 8, 2018, https://www.businesstoday.in/opinion/interviews/anand-mahindra-satyam-rise/story/18639.html.

manufactured Ford Escort to be the first people to work on Scorpio. He maintains that M&M would probably have been unable to design the Scorpio in its present form without the learning from the Ford JV.

JOINT VENTURES IN THE SOFTWARE SECTOR

Mr Anand Mahindra has also entered into JVs in software services. The group's JV with British Telecom in 1986 turned out to be fairly successful. However, in 2010, British Telecom reduced its stake to only 30 per cent. This created a dicey situation for M&M, as the group now had to hunt for other avenues to grow this company.

It was while M&M was grappling with the changing dynamics with British Telecom that the Satyam scandal broke out. Mr Anand Mahindra had been in the middle of discussions with Mr Raju, Chairman and CEO of Satyam, to explore possibilities of a merger. But as we discussed earlier, Mr Raju did not respond to his offer. When the scandal made it apparent that Satyam had been committing a series of frauds and misstating the sales figures, the Government of India stepped in to investigate the fraud. There was significant uncertainty regarding the future of the company. Many business houses might have chosen to steer clear of such a beleaguered association, but Mr Mahindra decided to go ahead with it. He reported being glad that he had managed to acquire Satyam through a transparent and fair process.

THE MAHINDRA-OLA DEAL: AGGRESSIVE, PROACTIVE COLLABORATION

In the 2000s, the automobile market in India started facing a serious challenge with the advent of start-ups like Uber and Ola. Services like these, where customers could avail of services like cab-hiring and ride-sharing, were swiftly becoming a global phenomenon, and India was not far behind. Soon, these firms threatened to replace conventional taxi services; they also became a threat to car ownership over time. So convenient and ubiquitous were these services that they made people reconsider using their private cars. While taxi services undoubtedly felt the brunt of this, car sales also plummeted with more and more people questioning the value of car ownership. Many major car players worldwide felt the impact affecting their businesses.

In September 2016, Mr Anand Mahindra partnered with Ola, an aggregator in India. It was a non-exclusive partnership under which M&M would provide 40,000 Veritos to Ola over two years. Drivers using the Ola platform could avail of low-cost financing, insurance and post-sales maintenance services as part of the Mahindra-Ola package. This partnership would translate into an additional $400 million worth of business by way of car purchases and financing services.

The Mahindra-Ola partnership showed not only foresight but also the clever grasp that Mr Anand Mahindra possessed over the changing business and social environment. He understood, far before many of his contemporaries did, that automobile manufacturers would *have* to collaborate with shared-ride aggregators to rise above the pitfalls of the transforming transportation scene in the country. In cementing this deal, Mr Mahindra once again charted out clear objectives that he also reiterated to the board:

- The partnership would put more cars on the road, thereby helping to minimize the pain point of not having enough cars available for these services.
- The M&M Group was positioned well enough to continue to make cars for the two emerging segments: one, the 'objects of desire', where the consumers would want to buy a car at any price, and two, the people who just needed access to a ride, with or without owning a car.

With the objectives well defined, Mr Mahindra directed his company's R&D team to focus on meeting the needs of both the segments identified above.[83] The Mahindra-Ola collaboration has since turned out to be a win-win for both parties.

---

[83] Samidha Sharma and Partha Shah, 'M&M to provide 40k cars to Ola, eyes $400m biz', *The Times of India*, September 9, 2016. Accessed on November 9, 2018. https://timesofindia.indiatimes.com/business/india-business/MM-to-provide-40k-cars-to-Ola-eyes-400m-biz/articleshow/54202026.cms

FORESIGHT IS PARAMOUNT TO A GOOD JOINT VENTURE

The one—and highly significant—takeaway from this chapter is the need to develop the clarity of purpose while entering into JVs. Business leaders need to look at JVs as strategic tools for growth, learning, or market entry/expansion. In fact, Mr Anand Mahindra's ability to grow with JVs (and acquisitions) has been one of the most important reasons behind M&M's spectacular growth.

However, in finalizing such deals, leaders must showcase foresight and a rock-solid understanding of exactly what the deal promises. For instance, in tying up with globally recognized players like Ford and Renault, Mr Mahindra had his intentions and objectives neatly pencilled out. In late 2018, M&M announced another tie-up with Ford. It can be assumed with considerable certainty that the purpose of this deal is crystal clear in the business plan of the man holding the reins.

Mr Anand Mahindra also understands that JVs are for a dual benefit; they are not tools to further ego or prestige. Making JVs work is a tough job, but it is one that has to be taken up by both parties. He encourages his people to learn quickly and dovetail their expertise in M&M as they did for the design and production of Scorpio.

16

THE SCORPIO STORY

LET'S DIVE INTO THE FASCINATING STORY OF SCORPIO; IT IS A TALE WITH ABUNDANT LEARNINGS THAT ALL BUSINESS PEOPLE SHOULD IMBIBE

By the year 1994, the M&M Group had become one of the largest tractor manufacturers internationally. Along with the Kubota Tractor Corporation of Japan and the Deere & Co. Company of the U.S., M&M was a sought-after, global tractor maker. The group had benefitted from incredible growth in India, which was the world's largest tractor market at the time.

To fuel its growth further, M&M had tied up with numerous companies for shared advantages. These included Peugeot, France and Tong Yang Moolsan Co. Ltd., Korea, which M&M partnered with for diesel engines and transmissions, and tractor transmission assemblies respectively.

In 1995, M&M entered into a JV with Ford to manufacture the Ford Escort for the Indian market. As we have seen previously, this agreement was dissolved in 1999. However, the experience that the M&M Group garnered from this association laid the ground for the development of Scorpio.

By 1997, Mr Mahindra had taken over as the MD of M&M. He swiftly restructured the group by retaining all the auto and tractor divisions but shifting the other business units into separate companies. He also undertook new hiring to channel talent into this restructured group. In 1993, Mr Mahindra hired Mr Pawan Goenka, who used to work with General Motors, to head the R&D unit of the M&M Group. His role entailed a complete and innovative focus on product development, which he performed with a team of 120 people. He led a young team (with an average age of twenty-seven years) and reported to Mr Alan Durante, the executive director of automobiles at the time.

We had discussed back in Chapter 6 how Mr Pawan Goenka eventually came up with two proposals: one, to improve the existing project that they were working on, or two, to develop new products. While Mr Anand Mahindra had already approached Ford to assist in new product development as part of their JV, Ford had only expressed interest in manufacturing. This could have been seen as a setback for new product development, with some business leaders probably choosing to drop the idea in favour of the first option (i.e. improving the existing product). However, Ford's refusal to assist in ideation turned out to be a blessing in disguise. Mr Mahindra observed in later years that it was a big favour that Ford did to the group, as M&M would have otherwise been dependent on Ford for technology and would have never been able to develop Scorpio.[84]

Excited and keen, Mr Anand Mahindra took the proposal to the board, stating his intentions to pursue the project and, if it so happened, for it to die a sudden death. This route, he surmised, would be preferable to dying a natural death that was almost certain if M&M did not initiate new product development.

The project involved several risks, some of which could endanger the future of the M&M Group. For one, it entailed an investment of ₹600 crore at a time when M&M's turnover was ₹4,000 crore and profits were ₹250 crore. Quite evidently, it was a gigantic financial risk. Moreover, the M&M Group had no experience in the SUV market, as they had always manufactured tractors and utility vehicles. The group's products were predominantly sold in rural markets. A Harvard Business School Case stated that an advertising professional once remarked, 'The name Mahindra was always associated with a jeep.'[85] In case the project failed for any reason, there was the hazard of losing the reputation that M&M had painstakingly built over the years.

---

[84] V. Keshavdev, 'The Boss Anand Mahindra', *Outlook Business*, July 10, 2015, accessed November 2018. https://www.outlookbusiness.com/specials/the-boss/anand-mahindra-1258

[85] Tarun Khanna, Rajiv Lal and Merina Manocaran, February 2005. 'M&M: Creating Scorpio', Harvard Business School Case, 705-478.

Despite the risks, Mr Anand Mahindra managed to get the proposal approved by the board; the members of the board are reported to have agreed primarily because of his commitment and passion towards the idea. Mr Mahindra also credits Mr Keshub Mahindra for his foresight in supporting the Scorpio project.

After receiving the green signal for the initiative, several immense tasks loomed in front of M&M. The company had to understand the demands and desires of the urban customer; previously, they had focused only on rural areas. The group also had to invest heavily in market research—a function that hadn't been truly employed before, as the company had been manufacturing products that were modified versions of the older models developed by their JV partners.

The company quickly rose to the occasion, setting into motion the following steps:

1. The M&M Group launched a modified version of the Armada, an SUV that the group had produced in India until 2001, to get customer feedback and announce their entry into the urban markets. It was called Bolero.
2. The group conducted market research to examine customer needs and figure out how to cater to them.
3. M&M worked closely with suppliers while designing new products to involve them early in the design process.
4. Finally, the group encouraged its vendors to choose

their collaborators. It also looked for component vendors in Asia, instead of Europe. This helped to reduce costs drastically, without compromising the quality of the products.

The above steps proved to be genuinely insightful in the course of product development. Mr Anand Mahindra also engaged some of the European suppliers who had followed the tracks of multinational car manufacturers in India and put up facilities to supply to them. But the demand was low, and most of these suppliers had huge unutilized capacities. Eager for new business, they were happy to help M&M with the Scorpio project, even though the project was considerably smaller in size than the ones they had been used to servicing.

Finally, when the Scorpio was launched in 2002, it proved to be a phenomenal success. The SUV had been developed at what was then the lowest cost, estimated at 10 per cent of what it would have cost a large manufacturer to produce. The instant success of the Scorpio catapulted M&M into the SUV arena and proved to the world that the group had the skills and the expertise to develop and launch a new vehicle. M&M exported the Scorpio to different countries around the world, including many in Western Europe. The risky bet that Mr Mahindra showed the willingness to wager and the effort put in by his committed team continues to pay rich dividends for the M&M Group even today.

DON'T LET PAST ACHIEVEMENTS BLIND YOU

The story of Scorpio is a heavyweight in the field of managerial learning—it is replete with classic lessons for business. But the most important takeaway, perhaps, is the sixth sense that a leader must develop to gauge the need for reinvention. Mr Anand Mahindra had the vision to understand that the M&M Group would need to innovate for long-term survival. During the conceptualization of Scorpio, M&M was in a dominant position as the manufacturer of tractors. It is possible that it could have continued to see steady sales in this sector, at least for the foreseeable future. However, Mr Mahindra showed the business acumen not to rest on one's laurels but ascertain profits for tomorrow, even though the present was already profitable. To guarantee its sectoral leadership, M&M had to diversify its product portfolio, and Mr Mahindra did not let the current success of his business blind him to this reality.

There was another trigger that prompted Mr Anand Mahindra to emphasize on the development of Scorpio: to achieve growth in a state of slow or nonexistent market growth. Let us understand this in some detail.

By 1994, M&M had already risen to the position of one of the world's largest tractor manufacturers. At this stage, additional growth would be tough. It would also be expensive. For a company with deep roots and considerable market leadership, every incremental step towards growth in market share comes at a high cost, especially if the competitors are also powerful. There are two possibilities in this situation:

1. **If the market is growing fast:** This situation is not an immediate challenge if the markets are growing rapidly, as in this scenario, there is enough potential for every player to grow. Major players can, at the very least, rise to the extent of the market. For example, if the market is expanding by 50 per cent, then a player can estimate that its growth can also be 50 per cent, providing no additional players enter the market.
2. **If the market is struggling with slow or zero growth:** If the market is not growing or expanding at a low rate, then the room for growth of the individual players becomes limited. Any player that aspires to develop needs to grab at someone else's market share. For example, if the markets are not growing and each player has a predetermined customer base, then a manufacturer's market share can increase only if someone else loses some of his shares. In the situation of a battle for market share, both players usually end up getting lower profits.

In the latter situation, it logically follows that a business house should look at new markets to become more profitable at lower costs. Since M&M was a locally established player in India, it had the advantage of being able to leverage some of its relationships with suppliers and other stakeholders as compared to global auto giants.

17
SUMMING UP: MANAGEMENT LESSONS FOR YOUR BUSINESS

In popular business literature and managerial circles, Mr Anand Mahindra is frequently called the 'Renaissance Man'. He is also titled the 'Federator'. The goodwill and repute that Mr Mahindra has earned have been the result of an eventful albeit challenging journey. He has been at the helm of his family's business since 1981, and, since then, has set in motion a unique trajectory of growth. Several of the initiatives he has taken have been diametrically different from the ones that had been prevalent in the company he had inherited.

In his journey so far as the MD and chairman of the M&M Group, Mr Anand Mahindra has faced numerous challenges and tricky situations, some of which have tested his capabilities to their limits. But this abundance of trials hasn't gotten him down; it has lent him the courage to tackle adversity. In fact, in the group's annual report of 2013, he joked about the battle he waged with hardships: even amid notorious tribulations, he had always managed to hold the steering wheel. Cynics might argue that Mr Mahindra had it all set out for him; after all, he had taken over a fairly successful family business. But the effort he has put in to grow the empire and increase it in scope as well as profitability by a huge margin cannot be denied. He has showcased the intuition and judgement to predict the challenges his company might face in the future and, along with his team, worked untiringly to implement steps to attend to these pronto. Let us recapitulate the management and business lessons we learnt from his journey.

1. Hire the people you can rely on during critical times

Mr Anand Mahindra has persevered to build an excellent team of professionals around him. This is true of the various companies that are part of the group. This committed team of professionals has helped him with major business decisions and provided the insight that has steered M&M towards success.

For instance, during the development of Scorpio, Mr Mahindra built a master team under Mr Alan Durante and Mr Pawan Goenka. The latter used to work in General Motors and had the necessary skill set to head the R&D division of M&M. Mr Mahindra empowered the new team with the budgets, approvals and encouragement that, in turn, resulted in the success of Scorpio. In hiring and training the right people, Mr Mahindra's dedication echoes the advice of Mr Peter Drucker. In Mr Drucker's book, *The Effective Executive*, Mr Jim Collins lucidly explains the guideline that Mr Drucker recommended for more capable human resources.

The accomplishments of a single right person in a key seat dwarf the combined accomplishment derived by dividing the seat among multiple B-players. Get better people, give them really big things to do, increase their responsibilities and let them work.[86]

2. Train your team so they can adapt to a changing environment

To ensure that his team remains top-notch and attuned to the changing diktats of the business environment, Mr Anand Mahindra invests considerably in their training and professional development. The employees of the M&M Group, although spread across the globe in diverse locations and cultural settings, are warmly integrated into the fast-growing company. They have access to the best B-schools and faculty.

3. Once you have a committed team of expert professionals, ensure to back them up

While the importance of having the right people for the job cannot be overstated, the team remains only as effective as its leader. Mr Anand Mahindra has ensured to invest

---

[86]Jim Collins, Foreword, Peter F. Drucker. *The Effective Executive*. 50th Edition, 2017.

complete trust in his expert team, after assuring himself of their capabilities. This support from the leader is not only a huge morale boost for the employees but also a terrific example of how all the cogs in the wheel are important to keep the business well oiled and running without glitches. Mr Mahindra believes in his team in the truest sense of the word and backs them right till the board level.

4. Be a good listener and encourage a free flow of ideas at all levels of the organization

Throughout his journey, Mr Anand Mahindra has kept himself disciplined, humble and open to new ideas. As a leader, he listens to his people and understands that the pivotal aspect of his role is to ensure that his group encourages innovation and free-flowing ideas. He is also perpetually on the alert, not hesitating to single out creative people within his organization and give them a separate sandbox in which to experiment. This helps protect the creativity from factors that could discourage its development.

It is crucial for a leader to promote an environment like this alongside ensuring that the organization has processes and operations in place. To further this, he has focused on improving the communication within the organization, making sure that all ideas are heard and discussed outside the proverbial silos. So, the ideas that have potential can be identified and thought through, and potential problems addressed early in the process.

5. Invest in new technologies, products and sectors that could serve as the engines of growth for the future

In the business world, as much as in any other aspect of life, permanence is illusory. The M&M Group has managed to build a solid core business and has continually focused on making it stronger. This has helped maintain the company's cash flows. However, Mr Anand Mahindra has shown the foresight to invest in newer technologies that could be the future engines of growth. This has often meant developing products today that could cannibalize the mainstream products of the company tomorrow, but this has not dissuaded him. The rationale driving this decision is one that business leaders need to keep in mind: it is better to cannibalize your products before your competitors trump it.

6. Don't hesitate to overhaul your organizational structure if you deem it essential to do so for future growth

Many managers endeavour to preserve past values and legacies of the organization in an attempt to keep its spirit intact. While this is important in essence, managers must also be able to harness the opportunities available in the present and take steps to keep the company relevant and profitable in the future.

Mr Anand Mahindra scrutinizes his organizational structure closely to assess if it needs change to fit with innovations and new ideas. If the corporate structure proves to be a limitation in achieving success, business leaders must not hesitate to find a way around it. This can be done by creating an environment where mavericks can innovate, without the fear of being stifled. If required, the organization can also be taken through an overhaul or rebranding.

This lesson is best learnt from the Scorpio project, wherein Mr Mahindra decided to build a dedicated team to design the product since M&M did not have the requisite design and development skills in-house. Scorpio was going to be a product with a predominantly urban focus, and M&M lacked the team or structure that could do it justice. Mr Mahindra could have outsourced the design, refreshed the design of an existing M&M product, or employed the services of Pininfarina S.p.A., the Italian design house he had bought in 2011. But he chose to break away from traditional methods and bring in a bold albeit risky structure whose payoffs would be bigger.

7. Trust in indigenous abilities for the development, production and sustenance of business

The unflinching trust that the M&M Group has shown in the indigenous development of automobiles has been the cornerstone of its progress. Mr Anand Mahindra has demonstrated that an Indian company can build new products and drive them to success, without having to depend on foreign manufacturers. A business needs to develop capabilities to operate by this mindset, and many of these require commitment and continuous funding over a long time. It is a strategy that may not find favour with investors, as results can take considerable time to start coming in. Stakeholders may not appreciate such investments either, especially when other, more lucrative opportunities with possibly higher returns are available. But Mr Mahindra, a long-term thinker, has relied on indigenous capabilities for several projects, and this has enabled his group to build a strong foundation on which to base its future.

8. To achieve what has never been seen before, make innovation your best friend. Discard rules that are counterproductive for the business

Today, a business house cannot flourish in the absence of innovation. Mr Anand Mahindra has proved to be a leader who promotes innovation by creating safe places for his people to experiment, independently from the overall systemic framework. M&M's pursuit of low costs may not have been possible had it followed only time-tested, traditional methods prevalent in the industry, and flinched at the idea of treading the path less trodden.

In fact, it is this tradition of innovation and not being afraid to bend the rules that also determined M&M's choice of vendors in crucial projects like the Scorpio. Mr Mahindra built trust in his vendors by allowing them to choose their collaborators. He well understood that to be competitive and cost-efficient, the company would have to rely on the expertise of the vendors. Consequently, he encouraged them to take responsibility for entire parts, even though some of them were handling such a responsibility for the first time. This is not to say that M&M cut corners in its quality standards; what it did was break away from the traditional path to achieve something new.

9. Know your weaknesses and work on them with humility, acquiring any knowledge you don't already possess from external sources if required

It is natural for successful companies to get swollen heads and assume that they are self-sufficient to deal with any new projects that come their way. When M&M was working on the Scorpio project, the team that was in charge of the R&D was extremely young; the average age was only twenty-seven years. This was a conscious decision, for Mr Anand Mahindra felt that a young team would be better equipped to identify the customers at whom Scorpio was targeted. M&M was predominantly present in rural areas at the time; it was here that it had its core strengths. But an SUV would need to attract the urban population whose needs M&M had yet to outline.

Mr Mahindra did not have the dangerous arrogance of assuming that his company's earlier experience of manufacturing Ford Escort would be adequate for this exercise. Instead, he had the humility to realize that M&M needed to get fresh knowledge. Moreover, M&M had previously manufactured products that were design modifications of the existing products of their JV partners. This was in contrast to the current project that required the company to design from the ground up, keeping the customers' needs in mind.

Therefore, Mr Mahindra set in place a team that worked on ferreting out valuable insights for the product. He also worked on revamping the marketing and distribution of the product, handpicking the showrooms in which to launch Scorpio.

10. Ensure smooth execution by streamlining the clauses of a project across the organization, including the board

In many companies, innovative teams succeed in coming up with groundbreaking ideas; only a handful of these companies manage to take these ideas to their deserved fulfilment. Mr Anand Mahindra, despite his strict focus on creativity and originality, appreciates that the biggest challenge is execution. Interestingly, flawless execution has become the secret sauce behind M&M's growth. While quite a few managers are able to draw out impressive strategies and plans, they flounder in their execution. Mr Mahindra, in his capacity as the MD and, subsequently, the chairman, has driven the spirit of execution across all the levels of the organization, personally ensuring that his team meets targets and commitments. Driving the agenda through to the board level takes considerable dedication and effort, especially to convince all the associated managers and unify them in approach. Business leaders and managers must develop a similar spirit of execution that gives everyone else in the company the determination to steer ideas to completion.

Mr Anand Mahindra is at the helm of the M&M Group; naturally, this is a position of great importance and responsibility. It is also a position of entitlement. Many business leaders get swayed by the overwhelming prestige value of a successful family-owned business, and this prevents them from taking strategic decisions for the growth of the empire. However, Mr Mahindra is a keen listener and a grounded, balanced leader. He has unwaveringly remained focused on growing his group by bolstering the core, seeking new opportunities, staying away from controversy, and showing brilliant judgement about issues that deserve and demand his commentary on public platforms.

In his capacity as the leader of a vast and imposing business empire, Mr Mahindra has kept his group indomitably on the path to success. By the looks of it, he has been laying the right foundation and building a robust institution that can face the vicissitudes of time. For the M&M Group, it seems highly probable, that the best days are yet to come.